Copyright © 2014 by

National Learning Corporation

212 Michael Drive, Syosset, New York 11791

All rights reserved, including the right of reproduction in whole or in part, in any form or by any means, electronic or mechanical, including photocopying, recording, or by any information storage and retrieval system, without permission in writing from the Publisher.

(516) 921-8888
(800) 645-6337
FAX: (516) 921-8743
www.passbooks.com
sales @ passbooks.com
info @ passbooks.com

PRINTED IN THE UNITED STATES OF AMERICA

PASSBOOK®

NOTICE

This book is SOLELY intended for, is sold ONLY to, and its use is RESTRICTED to *individual*, bona fide applicants or candidates who qualify by virtue of having seriously filed applications for appropriate license, certificate, professional and/or promotional advancement, higher school matriculation, scholarship, or other legitimate requirements of educational and/or governmental authorities.

This book is NOT intended for use, class instruction, tutoring, training, duplication, copying, reprinting, excerption, or adaptation, etc., by:

(1) Other publishers

(2) Proprietors and/or Instructors of "Coaching" and/or Preparatory Courses

(3) Personnel and/or Training Divisions of commercial, industrial, and governmental organizations

(4) Schools, colleges, or universities and/or their departments and staffs, including teachers and other personnel

(5) Testing Agencies or Bureaus

(6) Study groups which seek by the purchase of a single volume to copy and/or duplicate and/or adapt this material for use by the group as a whole without having purchased individual volumes for each of the members of the group

(7) Et al.

Such persons would be in violation of appropriate Federal and State statutes.

PROVISION OF LICENSING AGREEMENTS. — Recognized educational commercial, industrial, and governmental institutions and organizations, and others legitimately engaged in educational pursuits, including training, testing, and measurement activities, may address a request for a licensing agreement to the copyright owners, who will determine whether, and under what conditions, including fees and charges, the materials in this book may be used by them. In other words, a licensing facility exists for the legitimate use of the material in this book on other than an individual basis. However, it is asseverated and affirmed here that the material in this book *CANNOT* be used without the receipt of the express permission of such a licensing agreement from the Publishers.

NATIONAL LEARNING CORPORATION
212 Michael Drive
Syosset, New York 11791

Inquiries re licensing agreements should be addressed to:
The President
National Learning Corporation
212 Michael Drive
Syosset, New York 11791

ISBN 0-8373-0254-4

C-254   CAREER EXAMINATION SERIES

This is your PASSBOOK® for...

File Clerk

EAST NORTHPORT PUBLIC LIBRARY
EAST NORTHPORT, NEW YORK

Test Preparation Study Guide

Questions & Answers

NLC

NATIONAL LEARNING CORPORATION

PASSBOOK® SERIES

THE *PASSBOOK® SERIES* has been created to prepare applicants and candidates for the ultimate academic battlefield — the examination room.

At some time in our lives, each and every one of us may be required to take an examination — for validation, matriculation, admission, qualification, registration, certification, or licensure.

Based on the assumption that every applicant or candidate has met the basic formal educational standards, has taken the required number of courses, and read the necessary texts, the *PASSBOOK® SERIES* furnishes the one special preparation which may assure passing with confidence, instead of failing with insecurity. Examination questions — together with answers — are furnished as the basic vehicle for study so that the mysteries of the examination and its compounding difficulties may be eliminated or diminished by a sure method.

This book is meant to help you pass your examination provided that you qualify and are serious in your objective.

The entire field is reviewed through the huge store of content information which is succinctly presented through a provocative and challenging approach — the question-and-answer method.

A climate of success is established by furnishing the correct answers at the end of each test.

You soon learn to recognize types of questions, forms of questions, and patterns of questioning. You may even begin to anticipate expected outcomes.

You perceive that many questions are repeated or adapted so that you can gain acute insights, which may enable you to score many sure points.

You learn how to confront new questions, or types of questions, and to attack them confidently and work out the correct answers.

You note objectives and emphases, and recognize pitfalls and dangers, so that you may make positive educational adjustments.

Moreover, you are kept fully informed in relation to new concepts, methods, practices, and directions in the field.

You discover that you are actually taking the examination all the time: you are preparing for the examination by "taking" an examination, not by reading extraneous and/or supererogatory textbooks.

In short, this PASSBOOK®, used directedly, should be an important factor in helping you to pass your test.

FILE CLERK

DUTIES
Performs filing and various related record keeping functions and clerical work in an office.

SCOPE OF THE EXAMINATION
The written test will be designed to test for knowledge, skills, and/or abilities in such areas as:
1. Filing practices, indexing, sorting and cross-referencing; equipment and terminology;
2. Organizing data into tables and records; and
3. Understanding and interpreting written material.

HOW TO TAKE A TEST

I. YOU MUST PASS AN EXAMINATION

A. *WHAT EVERY CANDIDATE SHOULD KNOW*

Examination applicants often ask us for help in preparing for the written test. What can I study in advance? What kinds of questions will be asked? How will the test be given? How will the papers be graded?

As an applicant for a civil service examination, you may be wondering about some of these things. Our purpose here is to suggest effective methods of advance study and to describe civil service examinations.

Your chances for success on this examination can be increased if you know how to prepare. Those "pre-examination jitters" can be reduced if you know what to expect. You can even experience an adventure in good citizenship if you know why civil service exams are given.

B. *WHY ARE CIVIL SERVICE EXAMINATIONS GIVEN?*

Civil service examinations are important to you in two ways. As a citizen, you want public jobs filled by employees who know how to do their work. As a job seeker, you want a fair chance to compete for that job on an equal footing with other candidates. The best-known means of accomplishing this two-fold goal is the competitive examination.

Exams are widely publicized throughout the nation. They may be administered for jobs in federal, state, city, municipal, town or village governments or agencies.

Any citizen may apply, with some limitations, such as the age or residence of applicants. Your experience and education may be reviewed to see whether you meet the requirements for the particular examination. When these requirements exist, they are reasonable and applied consistently to all applicants. Thus, a competitive examination may cause you some uneasiness now, but it is your privilege and safeguard.

C. *HOW ARE CIVIL SERVICE EXAMS DEVELOPED?*

Examinations are carefully written by trained technicians who are specialists in the field known as "psychological measurement," in consultation with recognized authorities in the field of work that the test will cover. These experts recommend the subject matter areas or skills to be tested; only those knowledges or skills important to your success on the job are included. The most reliable books and source materials available are used as references. Together, the experts and technicians judge the difficulty level of the questions.

Test technicians know how to phrase questions so that the problem is clearly stated. Their ethics do not permit "trick" or "catch" questions. Questions may have been tried out on sample groups, or subjected to statistical analysis, to determine their usefulness.

Written tests are often used in combination with performance tests, ratings of training and experience, and oral interviews. All of these measures combine to form the best-known means of finding the right person for the right job.

II. HOW TO PASS THE WRITTEN TEST

A. NATURE OF THE EXAMINATION

To prepare intelligently for civil service examinations, you should know how they differ from school examinations you have taken. In school you were assigned certain definite pages to read or subjects to cover. The examination questions were quite detailed and usually emphasized memory. Civil service exams, on the other hand, try to discover your present ability to perform the duties of a position, plus your potentiality to learn these duties. In other words, a civil service exam attempts to predict how successful you will be. Questions cover such a broad area that they cannot be as minute and detailed as school exam questions.

In the public service similar kinds of work, or positions, are grouped together in one "class." This process is known as *position-classification*. All the positions in a class are paid according to the salary range for that class. One class title covers all of these positions, and they are all tested by the same examination.

B. FOUR BASIC STEPS

1) Study the announcement

How, then, can you know what subjects to study? Our best answer is: "Learn as much as possible about the class of positions for which you've applied." The exam will test the knowledge, skills and abilities needed to do the work.

Your most valuable source of information about the position you want is the official exam announcement. This announcement lists the training and experience qualifications. Check these standards and apply only if you come reasonably close to meeting them.

The brief description of the position in the examination announcement offers some clues to the subjects which will be tested. Think about the job itself. Review the duties in your mind. Can you perform them, or are there some in which you are rusty? Fill in the blank spots in your preparation.

Many jurisdictions preview the written test in the exam announcement by including a section called "Knowledge and Abilities Required," "Scope of the Examination," or some similar heading. Here you will find out specifically what fields will be tested.

2) Review your own background

Once you learn in general what the position is all about, and what you need to know to do the work, ask yourself which subjects you already know fairly well and which need improvement. You may wonder whether to concentrate on improving your strong areas or on building some background in your fields of weakness. When the announcement has specified "some knowledge" or "considerable knowledge," or has used adjectives like "beginning principles of…" or "advanced … methods," you can get a clue as to the number and difficulty of questions to be asked in any given field. More questions, and hence broader coverage, would be included for those subjects which are more important in the work. Now weigh your strengths and weaknesses against the job requirements and prepare accordingly.

3) Determine the level of the position

Another way to tell how intensively you should prepare is to understand the level of the job for which you are applying. Is it the entering level? In other words, is this the position in which beginners in a field of work are hired? Or is it an intermediate or advanced level? Sometimes this is indicated by such words as "Junior" or "Senior" in the class title. Other jurisdictions use Roman numerals to designate the level – Clerk I, Clerk II, for example. The word "Supervisor" sometimes appears in the title. If the level is not indicated by the title, check the description of duties. Will you be working under very close supervision, or will you have responsibility for independent decisions in this work?

4) Choose appropriate study materials

Now that you know the subjects to be examined and the relative amount of each subject to be covered, you can choose suitable study materials. For beginning level jobs, or even advanced ones, if you have a pronounced weakness in some aspect of your training, read a modern, standard textbook in that field. Be sure it is up to date and has general coverage. Such books are normally available at your library, and the librarian will be glad to help you locate one. For entry-level positions, questions of appropriate difficulty are chosen – neither highly advanced questions, nor those too simple. Such questions require careful thought but not advanced training.

If the position for which you are applying is technical or advanced, you will read more advanced, specialized material. If you are already familiar with the basic principles of your field, elementary textbooks would waste your time. Concentrate on advanced textbooks and technical periodicals. Think through the concepts and review difficult problems in your field.

These are all general sources. You can get more ideas on your own initiative, following these leads. For example, training manuals and publications of the government agency which employs workers in your field can be useful, particularly for technical and professional positions. A letter or visit to the government department involved may result in more specific study suggestions, and certainly will provide you with a more definite idea of the exact nature of the position you are seeking.

III. KINDS OF TESTS

Tests are used for purposes other than measuring knowledge and ability to perform specified duties. For some positions, it is equally important to test ability to make adjustments to new situations or to profit from training. In others, basic mental abilities not dependent on information are essential. Questions which test these things may not appear as pertinent to the duties of the position as those which test for knowledge and information. Yet they are often highly important parts of a fair examination. For very general questions, it is almost impossible to help you direct your study efforts. What we can do is to point out some of the more common of these general abilities needed in public service positions and describe some typical questions.

1) General information

Broad, general information has been found useful for predicting job success in some kinds of work. This is tested in a variety of ways, from vocabulary lists to questions about current events. Basic background in some field of work, such as sociology or economics, may be sampled in a group of questions. Often these are principles which have become familiar to most persons through exposure rather than through formal training. It is difficult to advise you how to study for these questions; being alert to the world around you is our best suggestion.

2) Verbal ability

An example of an ability needed in many positions is verbal or language ability. Verbal ability is, in brief, the ability to use and understand words. Vocabulary and grammar tests are typical measures of this ability. Reading comprehension or paragraph interpretation questions are common in many kinds of civil service tests. You are given a paragraph of written material and asked to find its central meaning.

3) Numerical ability

Number skills can be tested by the familiar arithmetic problem, by checking paired lists of numbers to see which are alike and which are different, or by interpreting charts and graphs. In the latter test, a graph may be printed in the test booklet which you are asked to use as the basis for answering questions.

4) Observation

A popular test for law-enforcement positions is the observation test. A picture is shown to you for several minutes, then taken away. Questions about the picture test your ability to observe both details and larger elements.

5) Following directions

In many positions in the public service, the employee must be able to carry out written instructions dependably and accurately. You may be given a chart with several columns, each column listing a variety of information. The questions require you to carry out directions involving the information given in the chart.

6) Skills and aptitudes

Performance tests effectively measure some manual skills and aptitudes. When the skill is one in which you are trained, such as typing or shorthand, you can practice. These tests are often very much like those given in business school or high school courses. For many of the other skills and aptitudes, however, no short-time preparation can be made. Skills and abilities natural to you or that you have developed throughout your lifetime are being tested.

Many of the general questions just described provide all the data needed to answer the questions and ask you to use your reasoning ability to find the answers. Your best preparation for these tests, as well as for tests of facts and ideas, is to be at your physical and mental best. You, no doubt, have your own methods of getting into an exam-taking mood and keeping "in shape." The next section lists some ideas on this subject.

IV. KINDS OF QUESTIONS

Only rarely is the "essay" question, which you answer in narrative form, used in civil service tests. Civil service tests are usually of the short-answer type. Full instructions for answering these questions will be given to you at the examination. But in case this is your first experience with short-answer questions and separate answer sheets, here is what you need to know:

1) **Multiple-choice Questions**

Most popular of the short-answer questions is the "multiple choice" or "best answer" question. It can be used, for example, to test for factual knowledge, ability to solve problems or judgment in meeting situations found at work.

A multiple-choice question is normally one of three types—
- It can begin with an incomplete statement followed by several possible endings. You are to find the one ending which *best* completes the statement, although some of the others may not be entirely wrong.
- It can also be a complete statement in the form of a question which is answered by choosing one of the statements listed.

- It can be in the form of a problem – again you select the best answer.

Here is an example of a multiple-choice question with a discussion which should give you some clues as to the method for choosing the right answer:

When an employee has a complaint about his assignment, the action which will *best* help him overcome his difficulty is to
   A. discuss his difficulty with his coworkers
   B. take the problem to the head of the organization
   C. take the problem to the person who gave him the assignment
   D. say nothing to anyone about his complaint

In answering this question, you should study each of the choices to find which is best. Consider choice "A" – Certainly an employee may discuss his complaint with fellow employees, but no change or improvement can result, and the complaint remains unresolved. Choice "B" is a poor choice since the head of the organization probably does not know what assignment you have been given, and taking your problem to him is known as "going over the head" of the supervisor. The supervisor, or person who made the assignment, is the person who can clarify it or correct any injustice. Choice "C" is, therefore, correct. To say nothing, as in choice "D," is unwise. Supervisors have and interest in knowing the problems employees are facing, and the employee is seeking a solution to his problem.

2) True/False Questions

The "true/false" or "right/wrong" form of question is sometimes used. Here a complete statement is given. Your job is to decide whether the statement is right or wrong.

SAMPLE: A roaming cell-phone call to a nearby city costs less than a non-roaming call to a distant city.

This statement is wrong, or false, since roaming calls are more expensive.
This is not a complete list of all possible question forms, although most of the others are variations of these common types. You will always get complete directions for answering questions. Be sure you understand *how* to mark your answers – ask questions until you do.

V. RECORDING YOUR ANSWERS

Computer terminals are used more and more today for many different kinds of exams.
For an examination with very few applicants, you may be told to record your answers in the test booklet itself. Separate answer sheets are much more common. If this separate answer sheet is to be scored by machine – and this is often the case – it is highly important that you mark your answers correctly in order to get credit.
An electronic scoring machine is often used in civil service offices because of the speed with which papers can be scored. Machine-scored answer sheets must be marked with a pencil, which will be given to you. This pencil has a high graphite content which responds to the electronic scoring machine. As a matter of fact, stray dots may register as answers, so do not let your pencil rest on the answer sheet while you are pondering the correct answer. Also, if your pencil lead breaks or is otherwise defective, ask for another.

Since the answer sheet will be dropped in a slot in the scoring machine, be careful not to bend the corners or get the paper crumpled.

The answer sheet normally has five vertical columns of numbers, with 30 numbers to a column. These numbers correspond to the question numbers in your test booklet. After each number, going across the page are four or five pairs of dotted lines. These short dotted lines have small letters or numbers above them. The first two pairs may also have a "T" or "F" above the letters. This indicates that the first two pairs only are to be used if the questions are of the true-false type. If the questions are multiple choice, disregard the "T" and "F" and pay attention only to the small letters or numbers.

Answer your questions in the manner of the sample that follows:

32. The largest city in the United States is
    A. Washington, D.C.
    B. New York City
    C. Chicago
    D. Detroit
    E. San Francisco

1) Choose the answer you think is best. (New York City is the largest, so "B" is correct.)
2) Find the row of dotted lines numbered the same as the question you are answering. (Find row number 32)
3) Find the pair of dotted lines corresponding to the answer. (Find the pair of lines under the mark "B.")
4) Make a solid black mark between the dotted lines.

VI. BEFORE THE TEST

Common sense will help you find procedures to follow to get ready for an examination. Too many of us, however, overlook these sensible measures. Indeed, nervousness and fatigue have been found to be the most serious reasons why applicants fail to do their best on civil service tests. Here is a list of reminders:

- Begin your preparation early – Don't wait until the last minute to go scurrying around for books and materials or to find out what the position is all about.
- Prepare continuously – An hour a night for a week is better than an all-night cram session. This has been definitely established. What is more, a night a week for a month will return better dividends than crowding your study into a shorter period of time.
- Locate the place of the exam – You have been sent a notice telling you when and where to report for the examination. If the location is in a different town or otherwise unfamiliar to you, it would be well to inquire the best route and learn something about the building.
- Relax the night before the test – Allow your mind to rest. Do not study at all that night. Plan some mild recreation or diversion; then go to bed early and get a good night's sleep.
- Get up early enough to make a leisurely trip to the place for the test – This way unforeseen events, traffic snarls, unfamiliar buildings, etc. will not upset you.
- Dress comfortably – A written test is not a fashion show. You will be known by number and not by name, so wear something comfortable.

- Leave excess paraphernalia at home – Shopping bags and odd bundles will get in your way. You need bring only the items mentioned in the official notice you received; usually everything you need is provided. Do not bring reference books to the exam. They will only confuse those last minutes and be taken away from you when in the test room.
- Arrive somewhat ahead of time – If because of transportation schedules you must get there very early, bring a newspaper or magazine to take your mind off yourself while waiting.
- Locate the examination room – When you have found the proper room, you will be directed to the seat or part of the room where you will sit. Sometimes you are given a sheet of instructions to read while you are waiting. Do not fill out any forms until you are told to do so; just read them and be prepared.
- Relax and prepare to listen to the instructions
- If you have any physical problem that may keep you from doing your best, be sure to tell the test administrator. If you are sick or in poor health, you really cannot do your best on the exam. You can come back and take the test some other time.

VII. AT THE TEST

The day of the test is here and you have the test booklet in your hand. The temptation to get going is very strong. Caution! There is more to success than knowing the right answers. You must know how to identify your papers and understand variations in the type of short-answer question used in this particular examination. Follow these suggestions for maximum results from your efforts:

1) Cooperate with the monitor

The test administrator has a duty to create a situation in which you can be as much at ease as possible. He will give instructions, tell you when to begin, check to see that you are marking your answer sheet correctly, and so on. He is not there to guard you, although he will see that your competitors do not take unfair advantage. He wants to help you do your best.

2) Listen to all instructions

Don't jump the gun! Wait until you understand all directions. In most civil service tests you get more time than you need to answer the questions. So don't be in a hurry. Read each word of instructions until you clearly understand the meaning. Study the examples, listen to all announcements and follow directions. Ask questions if you do not understand what to do.

3) Identify your papers

Civil service exams are usually identified by number only. You will be assigned a number; you must not put your name on your test papers. Be sure to copy your number correctly. Since more than one exam may be given, copy your exact examination title.

4) Plan your time

Unless you are told that a test is a "speed" or "rate of work" test, speed itself is usually not important. Time enough to answer all the questions will be provided, but this does not mean that you have all day. An overall time limit has been set. Divide the total time (in minutes) by the number of questions to determine the approximate time you have for each question.

5) Do not linger over difficult questions

If you come across a difficult question, mark it with a paper clip (useful to have along) and come back to it when you have been through the booklet. One caution if you do this – be sure to skip a number on your answer sheet as well. Check often to be sure that you have not lost your place and that you are marking in the row numbered the same as the question you are answering.

6) Read the questions

Be sure you know what the question asks! Many capable people are unsuccessful because they failed to *read* the questions correctly.

7) Answer all questions

Unless you have been instructed that a penalty will be deducted for incorrect answers, it is better to guess than to omit a question.

8) Speed tests

It is often better NOT to guess on speed tests. It has been found that on timed tests people are tempted to spend the last few seconds before time is called in marking answers at random – without even reading them – in the hope of picking up a few extra points. To discourage this practice, the instructions may warn you that your score will be "corrected" for guessing. That is, a penalty will be applied. The incorrect answers will be deducted from the correct ones, or some other penalty formula will be used.

9) Review your answers

If you finish before time is called, go back to the questions you guessed or omitted to give them further thought. Review other answers if you have time.

10) Return your test materials

If you are ready to leave before others have finished or time is called, take ALL your materials to the monitor and leave quietly. Never take any test material with you. The monitor can discover whose papers are not complete, and taking a test booklet may be grounds for disqualification.

VIII. EXAMINATION TECHNIQUES

1) Read the general instructions carefully. These are usually printed on the first page of the exam booklet. As a rule, these instructions refer to the timing of the examination; the fact that you should not start work until the signal and must stop work at a signal, etc. If there are any *special* instructions, such as a choice of questions to be answered, make sure that you note this instruction carefully.

2) When you are ready to start work on the examination, that is as soon as the signal has been given, read the instructions to each question booklet, underline any key words or phrases, such as *least*, *best*, *outline*, *describe* and the like. In this way you will tend to answer as requested rather than discover on reviewing your paper that you *listed without describing*, that you selected the *worst* choice rather than the *best* choice, etc.

3) If the examination is of the objective or multiple-choice type – that is, each question will also give a series of possible answers: A, B, C or D, and you are called upon to select the best answer and write the letter next to that answer on your answer paper – it is advisable to start answering each question in turn. There may be anywhere from 50 to 100 such questions in the three or four hours allotted and you can see how much time would be taken if you read through all the questions before beginning to answer any. Furthermore, if you come across a question or group of questions which you know would be difficult to answer, it would undoubtedly affect your handling of all the other questions.

4) If the examination is of the essay type and contains but a few questions, it is a moot point as to whether you should read all the questions before starting to answer any one. Of course, if you are given a choice – say five out of seven and the like – then it is essential to read all the questions so you can eliminate the two that are most difficult. If, however, you are asked to answer all the questions, there may be danger in trying to answer the easiest one first because you may find that you will spend too much time on it. The best technique is to answer the first question, then proceed to the second, etc.

5) Time your answers. Before the exam begins, write down the time it started, then add the time allowed for the examination and write down the time it must be completed, then divide the time available somewhat as follows:
    - If 3-1/2 hours are allowed, that would be 210 minutes. If you have 80 objective-type questions, that would be an average of 2-1/2 minutes per question. Allow yourself no more than 2 minutes per question, or a total of 160 minutes, which will permit about 50 minutes to review.
    - If for the time allotment of 210 minutes there are 7 essay questions to answer, that would average about 30 minutes a question. Give yourself only 25 minutes per question so that you have about 35 minutes to review.

6) The most important instruction is to *read each question* and make sure you know what is wanted. The second most important instruction is to *time yourself properly* so that you answer every question. The third most important instruction is to *answer every question*. Guess if you have to but include something for each question. Remember that you will receive no credit for a blank and will probably receive some credit if you write something in answer to an essay question. If you guess a letter – say "B" for a multiple-choice question – you may have guessed right. If you leave a blank as an answer to a multiple-choice question, the examiners may respect your feelings but it will not add a point to your score. Some exams may penalize you for wrong answers, so in such cases *only*, you may not want to guess unless you have some basis for your answer.

7) Suggestions
    a. Objective-type questions
        1. Examine the question booklet for proper sequence of pages and questions
        2. Read all instructions carefully
        3. Skip any question which seems too difficult; return to it after all other questions have been answered
        4. Apportion your time properly; do not spend too much time on any single question or group of questions

5. Note and underline key words – *all, most, fewest, least, best, worst, same, opposite,* etc.
6. Pay particular attention to negatives
7. Note unusual option, e.g., unduly long, short, complex, different or similar in content to the body of the question
8. Observe the use of "hedging" words – *probably, may, most likely,* etc.
9. Make sure that your answer is put next to the same number as the question
10. Do not second-guess unless you have good reason to believe the second answer is definitely more correct
11. Cross out original answer if you decide another answer is more accurate; do not erase until you are ready to hand your paper in
12. Answer all questions; guess unless instructed otherwise
13. Leave time for review

b. Essay questions
1. Read each question carefully
2. Determine exactly what is wanted. Underline key words or phrases.
3. Decide on outline or paragraph answer
4. Include many different points and elements unless asked to develop any one or two points or elements
5. Show impartiality by giving pros and cons unless directed to select one side only
6. Make and write down any assumptions you find necessary to answer the questions
7. Watch your English, grammar, punctuation and choice of words
8. Time your answers; don't crowd material

8) Answering the essay question

Most essay questions can be answered by framing the specific response around several key words or ideas. Here are a few such key words or ideas:

M's: manpower, materials, methods, money, management
P's: purpose, program, policy, plan, procedure, practice, problems, pitfalls, personnel, public relations

a. Six basic steps in handling problems:
1. Preliminary plan and background development
2. Collect information, data and facts
3. Analyze and interpret information, data and facts
4. Analyze and develop solutions as well as make recommendations
5. Prepare report and sell recommendations
6. Install recommendations and follow up effectiveness

b. Pitfalls to avoid
1. *Taking things for granted* – A statement of the situation does not necessarily imply that each of the elements is necessarily true; for example, a complaint may be invalid and biased so that all that can be taken for granted is that a complaint has been registered

2. *Considering only one side of a situation* – Wherever possible, indicate several alternatives and then point out the reasons you selected the best one
3. *Failing to indicate follow up* – Whenever your answer indicates action on your part, make certain that you will take proper follow-up action to see how successful your recommendations, procedures or actions turn out to be
4. *Taking too long in answering any single question* – Remember to time your answers properly

IX. AFTER THE TEST

Scoring procedures differ in detail among civil service jurisdictions although the general principles are the same. Whether the papers are hand-scored or graded by machine we have described, they are nearly always graded by number. That is, the person who marks the paper knows only the number – never the name – of the applicant. Not until all the papers have been graded will they be matched with names. If other tests, such as training and experience or oral interview ratings have been given, scores will be combined. Different parts of the examination usually have different weights. For example, the written test might count 60 percent of the final grade, and a rating of training and experience 40 percent. In many jurisdictions, veterans will have a certain number of points added to their grades.

After the final grade has been determined, the names are placed in grade order and an eligible list is established. There are various methods for resolving ties between those who get the same final grade – probably the most common is to place first the name of the person whose application was received first. Job offers are made from the eligible list in the order the names appear on it. You will be notified of your grade and your rank as soon as all these computations have been made. This will be done as rapidly as possible.

People who are found to meet the requirements in the announcement are called "eligibles." Their names are put on a list of eligible candidates. An eligible's chances of getting a job depend on how high he stands on this list and how fast agencies are filling jobs from the list.

When a job is to be filled from a list of eligibles, the agency asks for the names of people on the list of eligibles for that job. When the civil service commission receives this request, it sends to the agency the names of the three people highest on this list. Or, if the job to be filled has specialized requirements, the office sends the agency the names of the top three persons who meet these requirements from the general list.

The appointing officer makes a choice from among the three people whose names were sent to him. If the selected person accepts the appointment, the names of the others are put back on the list to be considered for future openings.

That is the rule in hiring from all kinds of eligible lists, whether they are for typist, carpenter, chemist, or something else. For every vacancy, the appointing officer has his choice of any one of the top three eligibles on the list. This explains why the person whose name is on top of the list sometimes does not get an appointment when some of the persons lower on the list do. If the appointing officer chooses the second or third eligible, the No. 1 eligible does not get a job at once, but stays on the list until he is appointed or the list is terminated.

X. HOW TO PASS THE INTERVIEW TEST

The examination for which you applied requires an oral interview test. You have already taken the written test and you are now being called for the interview test – the final part of the formal examination.

You may think that it is not possible to prepare for an interview test and that there are no procedures to follow during an interview. Our purpose is to point out some things you can do in advance that will help you and some good rules to follow and pitfalls to avoid while you are being interviewed.

What is an interview supposed to test?

The written examination is designed to test the technical knowledge and competence of the candidate; the oral is designed to evaluate intangible qualities, not readily measured otherwise, and to establish a list showing the relative fitness of each candidate – as measured against his competitors – for the position sought. Scoring is not on the basis of "right" and "wrong," but on a sliding scale of values ranging from "not passable" to "outstanding." As a matter of fact, it is possible to achieve a relatively low score without a single "incorrect" answer because of evident weakness in the qualities being measured.

Occasionally, an examination may consist entirely of an oral test – either an individual or a group oral. In such cases, information is sought concerning the technical knowledges and abilities of the candidate, since there has been no written examination for this purpose. More commonly, however, an oral test is used to supplement a written examination.

Who conducts interviews?

The composition of oral boards varies among different jurisdictions. In nearly all, a representative of the personnel department serves as chairman. One of the members of the board may be a representative of the department in which the candidate would work. In some cases, "outside experts" are used, and, frequently, a businessman or some other representative of the general public is asked to serve. Labor and management or other special groups may be represented. The aim is to secure the services of experts in the appropriate field.

However the board is composed, it is a good idea (and not at all improper or unethical) to ascertain in advance of the interview who the members are and what groups they represent. When you are introduced to them, you will have some idea of their backgrounds and interests, and at least you will not stutter and stammer over their names.

What should be done before the interview?

While knowledge about the board members is useful and takes some of the surprise element out of the interview, there is other preparation which is more substantive. It *is* possible to prepare for an oral interview – in several ways:

1) Keep a copy of your application and review it carefully before the interview

This may be the only document before the oral board, and the starting point of the interview. Know what education and experience you have listed there, and the sequence and dates of all of it. Sometimes the board will ask you to review the highlights of your experience for them; you should not have to hem and haw doing it.

2) Study the class specification and the examination announcement

Usually, the oral board has one or both of these to guide them. The qualities, characteristics or knowledges required by the position sought are stated in these documents. They offer valuable clues as to the nature of the oral interview. For example, if the job involves supervisory responsibilities, the announcement will usually indicate that knowledge of modern supervisory methods and the qualifications of the candidate as a supervisor will be tested. If so, you can expect such questions, frequently in the form of a hypothetical situation which you are expected to solve. NEVER go into an oral without knowledge of the duties and responsibilities of the job you seek.

3) Think through each qualification required

Try to visualize the kind of questions you would ask if you were a board member. How well could you answer them? Try especially to appraise your own knowledge and background in each area, *measured against the job sought*, and identify any areas in which you are weak. Be critical and realistic – do not flatter yourself.

4) Do some general reading in areas in which you feel you may be weak

For example, if the job involves supervision and your past experience has NOT, some general reading in supervisory methods and practices, particularly in the field of human relations, might be useful. Do NOT study agency procedures or detailed manuals. The oral board will be testing your understanding and capacity, not your memory.

5) Get a good night's sleep and watch your general health and mental attitude

You will want a clear head at the interview. Take care of a cold or any other minor ailment, and of course, no hangovers.

What should be done on the day of the interview?

Now comes the day of the interview itself. Give yourself plenty of time to get there. Plan to arrive somewhat ahead of the scheduled time, particularly if your appointment is in the fore part of the day. If a previous candidate fails to appear, the board might be ready for you a bit early. By early afternoon an oral board is almost invariably behind schedule if there are many candidates, and you may have to wait. Take along a book or magazine to read, or your application to review, but leave any extraneous material in the waiting room when you go in for your interview. In any event, relax and compose yourself.

The matter of dress is important. The board is forming impressions about you – from your experience, your manners, your attitude, and your appearance. Give your personal appearance careful attention. Dress your best, but not your flashiest. Choose conservative, appropriate clothing, and be sure it is immaculate. This is a business interview, and your appearance should indicate that you regard it as such. Besides, being well groomed and properly dressed will help boost your confidence.

Sooner or later, someone will call your name and escort you into the interview room. *This is it.* From here on you are on your own. It is too late for any more preparation. But remember, you asked for this opportunity to prove your fitness, and you are here because your request was granted.

What happens when you go in?

The usual sequence of events will be as follows: The clerk (who is often the board stenographer) will introduce you to the chairman of the oral board, who will introduce you to the other members of the board. Acknowledge the introductions before you sit down. Do not be surprised if you find a microphone facing you or a stenotypist sitting by. Oral interviews are usually recorded in the event of an appeal or other review.

Usually the chairman of the board will open the interview by reviewing the highlights of your education and work experience from your application – primarily for the benefit of the other members of the board, as well as to get the material into the record. Do not interrupt or comment unless there is an error or significant misinterpretation; if that is the case, do not hesitate. But do not quibble about insignificant matters. Also, he will usually ask you some question about your education, experience or your present job – partly to get you to start talking and to establish the interviewing "rapport." He may start the actual questioning, or turn it over to one of the other members. Frequently, each member undertakes the questioning on a particular area, one in which he is perhaps most competent, so you can expect each member to participate in the examination. Because time is limited, you may also expect some rather abrupt switches in the direction the questioning takes, so do not be upset by it. Normally, a board member will not pursue a single line of questioning unless he discovers a particular strength or weakness.

After each member has participated, the chairman will usually ask whether any member has any further questions, then will ask you if you have anything you wish to add. Unless you are expecting this question, it may floor you. Worse, it may start you off on an extended, extemporaneous speech. The board is not usually seeking more information. The question is principally to offer you a last opportunity to present further qualifications or to indicate that you have nothing to add. So, if you feel that a significant qualification or characteristic has been overlooked, it is proper to point it out in a sentence or so. Do not compliment the board on the thoroughness of their examination – they have been sketchy, and you know it. If you wish, merely say, "No thank you, I have nothing further to add." This is a point where you can "talk yourself out" of a good impression or fail to present an important bit of information. Remember, *you close the interview yourself.*

The chairman will then say, "That is all, Mr. _____, thank you." Do not be startled; the interview is over, and quicker than you think. Thank him, gather your belongings and take your leave. Save your sigh of relief for the other side of the door.

How to put your best foot forward
Throughout this entire process, you may feel that the board individually and collectively is trying to pierce your defenses, seek out your hidden weaknesses and embarrass and confuse you. Actually, this is not true. They are obliged to make an appraisal of your qualifications for the job you are seeking, and they want to see you in your best light. Remember, they must interview all candidates and a non-cooperative candidate may become a failure in spite of their best efforts to bring out his qualifications. Here are 15 suggestions that will help you:

1) Be natural – Keep your attitude confident, not cocky
If you are not confident that you can do the job, do not expect the board to be. Do not apologize for your weaknesses, try to bring out your strong points. The board is interested in a positive, not negative, presentation. Cockiness will antagonize any board member and make him wonder if you are covering up a weakness by a false show of strength.

2) Get comfortable, but don't lounge or sprawl
Sit erectly but not stiffly. A careless posture may lead the board to conclude that you are careless in other things, or at least that you are not impressed by the importance of the occasion. Either conclusion is natural, even if incorrect. Do not fuss with your clothing, a pencil or an ashtray. Your hands may occasionally be useful to emphasize a point; do not let them become a point of distraction.

3) Do not wisecrack or make small talk
This is a serious situation, and your attitude should show that you consider it as such. Further, the time of the board is limited – they do not want to waste it, and neither should you.

4) Do not exaggerate your experience or abilities

In the first place, from information in the application or other interviews and sources, the board may know more about you than you think. Secondly, you probably will not get away with it. An experienced board is rather adept at spotting such a situation, so do not take the chance.

5) If you know a board member, do not make a point of it, yet do not hide it

Certainly you are not fooling him, and probably not the other members of the board. Do not try to take advantage of your acquaintanceship – it will probably do you little good.

6) Do not dominate the interview

Let the board do that. They will give you the clues – do not assume that you have to do all the talking. Realize that the board has a number of questions to ask you, and do not try to take up all the interview time by showing off your extensive knowledge of the answer to the first one.

7) Be attentive

You only have 20 minutes or so, and you should keep your attention at its sharpest throughout. When a member is addressing a problem or question to you, give him your undivided attention. Address your reply principally to him, but do not exclude the other board members.

8) Do not interrupt

A board member may be stating a problem for you to analyze. He will ask you a question when the time comes. Let him state the problem, and wait for the question.

9) Make sure you understand the question

Do not try to answer until you are sure what the question is. If it is not clear, restate it in your own words or ask the board member to clarify it for you. However, do not haggle about minor elements.

10) Reply promptly but not hastily

A common entry on oral board rating sheets is "candidate responded readily," or "candidate hesitated in replies." Respond as promptly and quickly as you can, but do not jump to a hasty, ill-considered answer.

11) Do not be peremptory in your answers

A brief answer is proper – but do not fire your answer back. That is a losing game from your point of view. The board member can probably ask questions much faster than you can answer them.

12) Do not try to create the answer you think the board member wants

He is interested in what kind of mind you have and how it works – not in playing games. Furthermore, he can usually spot this practice and will actually grade you down on it.

13) Do not switch sides in your reply merely to agree with a board member

Frequently, a member will take a contrary position merely to draw you out and to see if you are willing and able to defend your point of view. Do not start a debate, yet do not surrender a good position. If a position is worth taking, it is worth defending.

14) Do not be afraid to admit an error in judgment if you are shown to be wrong

The board knows that you are forced to reply without any opportunity for careful consideration. Your answer may be demonstrably wrong. If so, admit it and get on with the interview.

15) Do not dwell at length on your present job

The opening question may relate to your present assignment. Answer the question but do not go into an extended discussion. You are being examined for a *new* job, not your present one. As a matter of fact, try to phrase ALL your answers in terms of the job for which you are being examined.

Basis of Rating

Probably you will forget most of these "do's" and "don'ts" when you walk into the oral interview room. Even remembering them all will not ensure you a passing grade. Perhaps you did not have the qualifications in the first place. But remembering them will help you to put your best foot forward, without treading on the toes of the board members.

Rumor and popular opinion to the contrary notwithstanding, an oral board wants you to make the best appearance possible. They know you are under pressure – but they also want to see how you respond to it as a guide to what your reaction would be under the pressures of the job you seek. They will be influenced by the degree of poise you display, the personal traits you show and the manner in which you respond.

ABOUT THIS BOOK

This book contains tests divided into Examination Sections. Go through each test, answering every question in the margin. We have also attached a sample answer sheet at the back of the book that can be removed and used. At the end of each test look at the answer key and check your answers. On the ones you got wrong, look at the right answer choice and learn. Do not fill in the answers first. Do not memorize the questions and answers, but understand the answer and principles involved. On your test, the questions will likely be different from the samples. Questions are changed and new ones added. If you understand these past questions you should have success with any changes that arise. Tests may consist of several types of questions. We have additional books on each subject should more study be advisable or necessary for you. Finally, the more you study, the better prepared you will be. This book is intended to be the last thing you study before you walk into the examination room. Prior study of relevant texts is also recommended. NLC publishes some of these in our Fundamental Series. Knowledge and good sense are important factors in passing your exam. Good luck also helps. So now study this Passbook, absorb the material contained within and take that knowledge into the examination. Then do your best to pass that exam.

EXAMINATION SECTION

BASIC FUNDAMENTALS OF FILING SCIENCE

TABLE OF CONTENTS

	Page
I. COMMENTARY	1
II. BASIS OF FILING	1
1. Types of Files	1
(1) Shannon File	1
(2) Spindle File	1
(3) Box File	1
(4) Flat File	1
(5) Bellows File	1
(6) Vertical File	1
(7) Clip File	1
(8) Visible File	1
(9) Rotary File	1
2. Aids in Filing	2
3. Variations of Filing Systems	2
4. Centralized Filing	2
5. Methods of Filing	2
(1) Alphabetic Filing	3
(2) Subject Filing	3
(3) Geographical File	3
(4) Chronological File	3
(5) Numerical File	3
6. Indexing	3
7. Alphabetizing	3
III. RULES FOR INDEXING AND ALPHABETIZING	3
IV. OFFICIAL EXAMINATION DIRECTIONS AND RULES	7
Official Directions	8
Official Rules for Alphabetical Filing	8
Names of Individuals	8
Names of Business Organizations	8
Sample Question	8

BASIC FUNDAMENTALS OF FILING SCIENCE

I. COMMENTARY

Filing is the systematic arrangement and storage of papers, cards, forms, catalogues, etc., so that they may be found easily and quickly. The importance of an efficient filing system cannot be emphasized too strongly. The filed materials form records which may be needed quickly to settle questions that may cause embarrassing situations if such evidence is not available. In addition to keeping papers in order so that they are readily available, the filing system must also be designed to keep papers in good condition. A filing system must be planned so that papers may be filed easily, withdrawn easily, and as quickly returned to their proper place. The cost of a filing system is also an important factor.

The need for a filing system arose when the business man began to carry on negotiations on a large scale. He could no longer be intimate with the details of his business. What was needed in the early era was a spindle or pigeon-hole desk. Filing in pigeon-hole desks is now almost completely extinct. It was an unsatisfactory practice since pigeon holes were not labeled, and the desk was an untidy mess.

II. BASIS OF FILING

The science of filing is an exact one and entails a thorough understanding of basic facts, materials, and methods. An overview of this important information now follows.

1. <u>Types of files</u>

   (1) *SHANNON FILE*

   This consists of a board, at one end of which are fastened two arches which may be opened laterally.

   (2) *SPINDLE FILE*

   This consists of a metal or wood base to which is attached a long, pointed spike. Papers are pushed down on the spike as received. This file is useful for temporary retention of papers.

   (3) *BOX FILE*

   This is a heavy cardboard or metal box, opening from the side like a book.

   (4) *FLAT FILE*

   This consists of a series of shallow drawers or trays, arranged like drawers in a cabinet.

   (5) *BELLOWS FILE*

   This is a heavy cardboard container with alphabetized or compartment sections, the ends of which are closed in such a manner that they resemble an accordion.

   (6) *VERTICAL FILE*

   This consists of one or more drawers in which the papers are stood on edge, usually in folders, and are indexed by guides. A series of two or more drawers in one unit is the usual file cabinet.

   (7) *CLIP FILE*

   This file has a large clip attached to a board and is very similar to the *SHANNON FILE*.

   (8) *VISIBLE FILE*

   Cards are filed flat in an overlapping arrangement which leaves a part of each card visible at all times.

   (9) *ROTARY FILE*

The *ROTARY FILE* has a number of visible card files attached to a post around which they can be revolved. The wheel file has visible cards which rotate around a horizontal axle.

   (10) TICKLER FILE

   This consists of cards or folders marked with the days of the month, in which materials are filed and turned up on the appropriate day of the month.

2. <u>Aids in filing</u>

   (1) GUIDES

   Guides are heavy cardboard, pasteboard, or bristol-board sheets the same size as folders. At the top is a tab on which is marked or printed the distinguishing letter, words, or numbers indicating the material filed in a section of the drawer.

   (2) SORTING TRAYS

   Sorting trays are equipped with alphabetical guides to facilitate the sorting of papers preparatory to placing them in a file.

   (3) CODING

   Once the classification or indexing caption has been determined, it must be indicated on the letter for filing purposes.

   (4) CROSS REFERENCE

   Some letters or papers might easily be called for under two or more captions. For this purpose, a cross-reference card or sheet is placed in the folder or in the index.

3. <u>Variations of filing systems</u>

   (1) VARIADEX ALPHABETIC INDEX

   Provides for more effective expansion of the alphabetic system.

   (2) TRIPLE-CHECK NUMERIC FILING

   Entails a multiple cross-reference, as the name implies.

   (3) VARIADEX FILING

   Makes use of color as an aid in filing.

   (4) DEWEY DECIMAL SYSTEM

   The system is a numeric one used in libraries or for filing library materials in an office. This special type of filing system is used where material is grouped in finely divided categories, such as in libraries. With this method, all material to be filed is divided into ten major groups, from 000 to 900, and then subdivided into tens, units, and decimals.

4. <u>Centralized filing</u>

   Centralized filing means keeping the files in one specific or central location. Decentralized filing means putting away papers in files of individual departments. The first step in the organization of a central filing department is to make a careful canvass of all desks in the offices. In this manner we can determine just what material needs to be filed, and what information each desk occupant requires from the central file. Only papers which may be used at some time by persons in the various offices should be placed in the central file. A paper that is to be used at some time by persons in the various offices should be placed in the central file. A paper that is to be used by one department only should never be filed in the central file.

5. <u>Methods of filing</u>

   While there are various methods used for filing, actually there are only five basic systems: alphabetical, subject, numerical, geographic, and chronological. All other systems are derived from one of these or from a combination of two or more of them.

Since the purpose of a filing system is to store business records <u>systemically</u> so that any particular record can be found almost instantly when required, filing requires, in addition to the proper kinds of equipment and supplies, an effective method of indexing.

There are five basic systems of filing:

(1) ALPHABETIC FILING

Most filing is alphabetical. Other methods, as described below, require extensive alphabetization.

In alphabetic filing, lettered dividers or guides are arranged in alphabetic sequence. Material to be filed is placed behind the proper guide. All materials under each letter are also arranged alphabetically. Folders are used unless the file is a card index.

(2) SUBJECT FILING

This method is used when a single, complete file on a certain subject is desired. A subject file is often maintained to assemble all correspondence on a certain subject. Such files are valuable in connection with insurance claims, contract negotiations, personnel, and other investigations, special programs, and similar subjects.

(3) GEOGRAPHICAL FILE

Materials are filed according to location: states, cities, counties, or other subdivisions. Statistics and tax information are often filed in this manner.

(4) CHRONOLOGICAL FILE

Records are filed according to date. This method is used especially in "tickler" files that have guides numbered 1 to 31 for each day of the month. Each number indicates the day of the month when the filed item requires attention.

(5) NUMERICAL FILE

This method requires an alphabetic card index giving name and number. The card index is used to locate records numbered consecutively in the files according to date received or sequence in which issued, such as licenses, permits, etc.

6. <u>Indexing</u>

Determining the name or title under which an item is to be filed is known as <u>indexing</u>. For example, how would a letter from Robert E. Smith be filed? The name would be rearranged Smith,Robert E., so that the letter would be filed under the last name.

7. <u>Alphabetizing</u>

The arranging of names for filing is known as <u>alphabetizing</u>. For example, suppose you have four letters indexed under the names Johnson, Becker, Roe, and Stern. How should these letters be arranged in the files so that they may be found easily? You would arrange the four names alphabetically, thus, Becker, Johnson, Roe, and Stern.

III. RULES FOR INDEXING AND ALPHABETIZING
  1. The names of persons are to be transposed. Write the surname first, then the given name, and, finally, the middle name or initial. Then arrange the various names according to the alphabetic order of letters throughout the entire name. If there is a title, consider that after the middle name or initial.

NAMES	INDEXED AS
Arthur L.Bright	Bright, Arthur L.
Arthur S.Bright	Bright, Arthur S.
P.E. Cole	Cole, P.E.

| Dr. John C. Fox | Fox, John C. (Dr.) |

2. If a surname includes the same letters of another surname, with one or more additional letters added to the end, the shorter surname is placed first regardless of the given name or the initial of the given name.

NAMES	INDEXED AS
Robert E. Brown	Brown, Robert E.
Gerald A. Browne	Browne, Gerald A.
William O. Brownell	Brownell, William O.

3. Firm names are alphabetized under the surnames. Words like the, an, a, of, and for, are not considered.

NAMES	INDEXED AS
Bank of America	Bank of America
Bank Discount Dept.	Bank Discount Dept.
The Cranford Press	Cranford Press, The
Nelson Dwyer & Co.	Dwyer, Nelson, & Co.
Sears, Roebuck & Co.	Sears, Roebuck & Co.
Montgomery Ward & Co.	Ward, Montgomery, & Co.

4. The order of filing is determined first of all by the first letter of the names to be filed. If the first letters are the same, the order is determined by the second letters, and so on. In the following pairs of names, the order is determined by the letters underlined:

A̲usten   Ha̲yes   Ha_n_son   Har_v_ey   Heat_h_   Gree_n_   Schwar_t_z
B̲aker   He̲ath   Ha_r_per   Har_w_ood Heat_o_n Green_e_ Schwar_z_

5. When surnames are alike, those with initials only precede those with given names, unless the first initial comes alphabetically after the first letter of the name.

Gleason, S.	*but,*	Abbott, Mary
Gleason, S.W.		Abbott, W.B.
Gleason, Sidney		

6. Hyphenated names are treated as if spelled without the hyphen.

| Lloyd, Paul N. | Lloyd, Robert |
| Lloyd-Jones, James | Lloyd-Thomas, A.S. |

7. Company names composed of single letters which are not used as abbreviations precede the other names beginning with the same letter.

B & S Garage	E Z Duplicator Co.
B X Cable Co.	Eagle Typewriter Co.
Babbitt, R.N.	Edison Company

8. The ampersand (&) and the apostrophe (') in firm names are disregarded in alphabetizing.

Nelson & Niller	M & C Amusement Corp.
Nelson, Walter J.	M C Art Assn.
Nelson's Bakery	

9. Names beginning with Mac, Mc, or M' are usually placed in regular order as spelled. Some filing systems file separately names beginning with Mc.

MacDonald, R.J.	Mazza, Anthony
Macdonald, S.B.	McAdam, Wm.
Mace, Wm.	McAndrews, Jerry

10. Names beginning with St. are listed as if the name Saint were spelled in full. Numbered street names and all abbreviated names are treated as if spelled out in full.

Saginaw	Fifth Avenue Hotel	Hart Mfg. Co.
St. Louis	42nd Street Dress Shop	Hart, Martin
St. Peter's Rectory	Hart, Chas.	Hart, Thos.

Sandford	Hart, Charlotte	Hart, Thomas A.
Smith, Wm.	Hart, Jas.	Hart, Thos. R.
Smith, Willis	Hart, Janice	

11. Federal, state, or city departments of government should be placed alphabetically under the governmental branch controlling them.

    Illinois, State of -- Departments and Commissions
        Banking Dept.
        Employment Bureau
    United States Government Departments
        Commerce
        Defense
        State
        Treasury

12. Alphabetic order

    Each word in a name is an indexing unit. Arrange the names in alphabetic order by comparing similar units in each name. Consider the second units only when the first units are identical. Consider the third units only when both the first and second units are identical.

13. Single surnames or initials

    A surname, when used alone, precedes the same surname with a first name or initial. A surname with a first initial only precedes a surname with a complete first name. This rule is sometimes stated, "nothing comes before something."

14. Surname prefixes

    A surname prefix is not a separate indexing unit, but it is considered part of the surname. These prefixes include: d', D', Da, de, De, Del, Des, Di, Du, Fitz., La, Le, Mc, Mac, 'c, O', St., Van, Van der, Von, Von der, and others. The prefixes M', Mac, and Mc are indexed and filed exactly as they are spelled.

15. Names of firms

    Names of firms and institutions are indexed and filed exactly as they are written when they do not contain the complete name of an individual.

16. Names of firms containing complete individual names

    When the firm or institution name includes the complete name of an individual, the units are transposed for indexing in the same way as the name of an individual.

17. Article "The"

    When the article the occurs at the beginning of a name, it is placed at the end in parentheses but it is not moved. In both cases, it is not an indexing unit and is disregarded in filing.

18. Hyphenated names

    Hyphenated firm names are considered as separate indexing units. Hyphenated surnames of individuals are considered as one indexing unit; this applies also to hyphenated names of individuals whose complete names are part of a firm name.

19. Abbreviations

    Abbreviations are considered as though the name were written in full; however, single letters other than abbreviations are considered as separate indexing units.

20. Conjunctions, prepositions and firm endings

    Conjunctions and prepositions, such as and, for, in, of, are disregarded in indexing and filing but are not omitted or their order changed when writing names on cards and folders. Firm endings, such as Ltd., Inc., Co., Son, Bros., Mfg., and Corp., are treated as a unit in indexing and filing and are considered as though spelled in full, such as Brothers and Incorporated.

21. One or two words

    Names that may be spelled either as one or two words are indexed and filed as one word.

22. Compound geographic names

    Compound geographic names are considered as separate indexing and filing units, except when the first part of the name is not an English word, such as the Los in Los Angeles.

23. Titles or degrees of individuals, whether preceding or following the name, are not considered in indexing or filing. They are placed in parentheses after the given name or initial. Terms that designate seniority, such as Jr., Sr., 2d, are also placed in parentheses and are considered for indexing and filing only when the names to be indexed are otherwise identical.

    Exception A:

    When the name of an individual consists of a title and one name only, such as Queen Elizabeth, it is not transposed and the title is considered for indexing and filing.

    Exception B:

    When a title or foreign article is the initial word of a firm or association name, it is considered for indexing and filing.

24. Possessives

    When a word ends in apostrophe s, the s is not considered in indexing and filing. However, when a word ends in s apostrophe, because the s is part of the original word, it is considered. This rule is sometimes stated, "Consider everything up to the apostrophe."

25. United States and foreign government names

    Names pertaining to the federal government are indexed and filed under United States Government and then subdivided by title of the department, bureau, division, commission, or board. Names pertaining to foreign governments are indexed and filed under names of countries and then subdivided by title of the department, bureau, division, commission, or board. Phrases, such as department of, bureau of, division of, commission of, board of, when used in titles of governmental bodies, are placed in parentheses after the word they modify, but are disregarded in indexing and filing. Such phrases, however, are considered in indexing and filing nongovernmental names.

26. Other political subdivisions

    Names pertaining to other political subdivisions, such as states, counties, cities, or towns, are indexed and filed under the name of the political subdivision and then subdivided by the title of the department, bureau, division, commission, or board.

27. Addresses

    When the same name appears with different addresses, the names are indexed as usual and arranged alphabetically according to city or town. The State is considered only when there is duplication of both individual or company name and city name. If the same name is located at different addresses within the same city, then the names are arranged alphabetically by streets. If the same name is located at more than one address on the same street, then the names are arranged from the lower to the higher street number.

28. Numbers

    Any number in a name is considered as though it were written in words, and it is indexed and filed as one unit.

29. Bank names
   Because the names of many banking institutions are alike in several respects, as first National Bank, Second National Bank, etc., banks are indexed and filed first by city location, then by bank name, with the state location written in parentheses and considered only if necessary
30. Married women
   The legal name of a married woman is the one used for filing purposes. Legally, a man's surname is the only part of a man's name a woman assumes when she marries. Her legal name, therefore, could be either:
   (1) Her own first and middle names together with her husband's surname, or
   (2) Her own first name and maiden surname, together with her husband's surname.
   Mrs. is placed in parentheses at the end of the name. Her husband's first and middle names are given in parentheses below her legal name.
31. An alphabetically arranged list of names illustrating many difficult points of alphabetizing follows.

COLUMN I	COLUMN II
Abbot , W.B.	54th St. Tailor Shop
Abbott, Alice	Forstall, W.J.
Allen, Alexander B.	44th St. Garage
Allen, Alexander B., Inc.	M A Delivery Co.
Andersen, Hans	M & C Amusement Corp.
Andersen, Hans E.	M C Art Assn.
Andersen, Hans E., Jr.	MacAdam, Wm.
Anderson, Andrew Andrews,	Macaulay, James
George Brown Motor Co., Boston	MacAulay, Wilson
Brown Motor Co., Chicago	MacDonald, R.J.
Brown Motor Co., Philadelphia	Macdonald, S.B.
Brown Motor Co., San Francisco	Mace, Wm.
Dean, Anna	Mazza, Anthony
Dean, Anna F.	McAdam, Wm.
Dean, Anna Frances	McAndrews, Jerry
Dean & Co.	Meade & Clark Co.
Deane-Arnold Apartments	Meade, S.T.
Deane's Pharmacy	Meade, Solomon
Deans, Felix A.	Sackett Publishing Co.
Dean's Studio	Sacks, Robert
Deans, Wm.	St.Andrew Hotel
Deans & Williams	St.John, Homer W.
East Randolph	Saks, Isaac B.
East St.Louis	Stephens, Ira
Easton, Pa.	Stevens, Delevan
Eastport, Me.	Stevens, Delila

IV. OFFICIAL EXAMINATION DIRECTIONS AND RULES
   To preclude the possibility of conflicting or varying methods of filing, explicit directions and express rules are given to the candidate before he answers the filing questions on an examination.
   The most recent official directions and rules for the filing questions are given immediately hereafter.

OFFICIAL DIRECTIONS

Each of questions ... to ... consists of four(five)names. For each question, select the one of the four(five)names that should be first (second)(third)(last) if the four(five)names were arranged in alphabetical order in accordance with the rules for alphabetical filing given below. Read these rules carefully. Then, for each question, indicate in the correspondingly numbered row on the answer sheet the letter preceding the name that should be first(second)(third)(last) in alphabetical order.

OFFICIAL RULES FOR ALPHABETICAL FILING

Names of Individuals

1. The names of individuals are filed in strict alphabetical order, first according to the last name, then according to first name or initial, and, finally, according to middle name or initial. For example: William Jones precedes George Kirk and Arthur S. Blake precedes Charles M. Blake.
2. When the last names are identical, the one with an initial instead of a first name precedes the one "with a first name beginning with the same initial. For example: J.Green precedes Joseph Green.
3. When identical last names also have identical first names, the one without a middle name or initial precedes the one with a middle name or initial. For example:Robert Jackson precedes both Robert C.Jackson and Robert Chester Jackson.
4. When last names are identical and the first names are also identical, the one with a middle initial precedes the one with a middle name beginning with the same initial. For example: Peter A. Brown precedes Peter Alvin Brown.
5. Prefixes such as De, El, La, and Van are considered parts of the names they precede. For example:Wilfred DeWald precedes Alexander Duval.
6. Last names beginning with "Mac" or "Mc" are filed as spelled.
7. Abbreviated names are treated as if they were spelled out. For example: Jos. is filed as Joseph and Robt. is filed as Robert.
8. Titles and designations such as Dr. ,Mrs., Prof. are disregarded in filing.

Names of Business Organizations

1. The names of business organizations are filed exactly as written, except that an organization bearing the name of an individual is filed alphabetically according to the name of the individual in accordance with the rules for filing names of individuals given above. For example: Thomas Allison Machine Company precedes Northern Baking Company.
2. When numerals occur in a name, they are treated as if they were spelled out. For example: 6 stands for six and 4th stands for fourth.
3. When the following words occur in names, they are disregarded: the, of, and Sample: Choose the name that should be filed *third*.

   (A) Fred Town   (2)   (C) D. Town   (1)
   (B) Jack Towne   (3)   (D) Jack S.Towne (4)

The numbers in parentheses indicate the proper alphabetical order in which these names should be filed. Since the name that should be filed <u>third</u> is Jack Towne, the answer is (B).

FILING

EXAMINATION SECTION
TEST 1

DIRECTIONS: Each question from 1 through 10 contains four names. For each question, choose the name that should be FIRST if the four names were arranged in alphabetical order in accordance with the Rules for Alphabetical Filing given before. Read these rules carefully. Then, for each question, print in the space at the right the letter before the name that should be FIRST in alphabetical order.

SAMPLE QUESTION
- A. Jane Earl (2)
- B. James A. Earle (4)
- C. James Earl (1)
- D. J. Earle (3)

The numbers in parentheses show the proper alphabetical order in which these names should be filed. Since the name that should be filed FIRST is James Earl, the answer to the sample question is C.

1. A. Majorca Leather Goods
   B. Robert Maiorca and Sons
   C. Maintenance Management Corp.
   D. Majestic Carpet Mills

   1.____

2. A. Municipal Telephone Service
   B. Municipal Reference Library
   C. Municipal Credit Union
   D. Municipal Broadcasting System

   2.____

3. A. Robert B. Pierce   B. R. Bruce Pierce
   C. Ronald Pierce   D. Robert Bruce Pierce

   3.____

4. A. Four Seasons Sports Club
   B. 14 Street Shopping Center
   C. Forty Thieves Restaurant
   D. 42nd St. Theaters

   4.____

5. A. Franco Franceschini   B. Amos Franchini
   C. Sandra Franceschia   D. Lilie Franchinesca

   5.____

6. A. Chas. A. Levine   B. Kurt Levene
   C. Charles Levine   D. Kurt E. Levene

   6.____

7. A. Prof. Geo. Kinkaid   B. Mr. Alan Kinkaid
   C. Dr. Albert A. Kinkade   D. Kincade Liquors Inc.

   7.____

8. A. Department of Public Events 8.____
   B. Office of the Public Administrator
   C. Queensborough Public Library
   D. Department of Public Health

9. A. Martin Luther King, Jr. Towers 9.____
   B. Metro North Plaza
   C. Manhattanville Houses
   D. Marble Hill Houses

10. A. Dr. Arthur Davids 10.____
    B. The David Check Cashing Service
    C. A. C. Davidsen
    D. Milton Davidoff

KEY (CORRECT ANSWERS)

1. C
2. D
3. B
4. D
5. C

6. B
7. D
8. B
9. A
10. B

TEST 2

DIRECTIONS: Each of questions 1 to 10 consists of four names. For each question, select the one of the four names that should be THIRD if the four names were arranged in alphabetical order in accordance with the Rules of Alphabetical Filing given before. Read these rules carefully. Then, for each question, print in the space at the right the letter preceding the name that should be THIRD in alphabetical order.

SAMPLE QUESTION

    A. Fred Town   (2)
    B. Jack Towne   (3)
    C. D. Town   (1)
    D. Jack S. Towne   (4)

The numbers in parentheses indicate the proper alphabetical order in which these names should be filed. Since the name that should be filed THIRD is Jack Towne, the answer is B.

1.   A. Herbert Restman   B. H. Restman   1.____
     C. Harry Restmore   D. H. Restmore

2.   A. Martha Eastwood   B. Martha E. Eastwood   2.____
     C. Martha Edna Eastwood   D. M. Eastwood

3.   A. Timothy Macalan   B. Fred McAlden   3.____
     C. Thomas MacAllister   D. Mrs. Frank McAllen

4.   A. Elm Trading Co.   4.____
     B. El Dorado Trucking Corp.
     C. James Eldred Jewelry Store
     D. Eldridge Printing, Inc.

5.   A. Edward La Gabriel   B. Marie Doris Gabriel   5.____
     C. Marjorie N. Gabriel   D. Mrs. Marian Gabriel

6.   A. Peter La Vance   B. George Van Meer   6.____
     C. Wallace De Vance   D. Leonard Vance

7.   A. Fifth Avenue Book Shop   7.____
     B. Mr. Wm. A. Fifner
     C. 52nd Street Association
     D. Robert B. Fiffner

8.   A. Dr. Chas. D. Peterson   B. Miss Irene F. Petersen   8.____
     C. Lawrence E. Peterson   D. Prof. N. A. Petersen

9.   A. 71st Street Theater   B. The Seven Seas Corp.   9.____
     C. 7th Ave. Service Co.   D. Walter R. Sevan and Co.

10. A. Aerol Auto Body, Inc. 10._____
    B. AAB Automotive Service Corp.
    C. Acer Automotive
    D. Alerte Automotive Corp.

KEY (CORRECT ANSWERS)

1. D
2. B
3. B
4. D
5. C

6. D
7. A
8. A
9. C
10. A

TEST 3

DIRECTIONS: Same as for Test 2.

1.	A.	William Carver	B.	Howard Cambell	1. ____
	C.	Arthur Chambers	D.	Charles Banner	
2.	A.	Paul Moore	B.	William Moore	2. ____
	C.	Paul A. Moore	D.	William Allen Moore	
3.	A.	George Peters	B.	Eric Petersen	3. ____
	C.	G. Peters	D.	E. Petersen	
4.	A.	Edward Hallam	B.	Jos. Frank Hamilton	4. ____
	C.	Edward A. Hallam	D.	Joseph F. Hamilton	
5.	A.	Theodore Madison	B.	Timothy McGill	5. ____
	C.	Thomas MacLane	D.	Thomas A. Madison	
6.	A.	William O'Hara	B.	Arthur Gordon	6. ____
	C.	James DeGraff	D.	Anne von Glatin	
7.	A.	Charles Green	B.	Chas. T. Greene	7. ____
	C.	Charles Thomas Greene	D.	Wm. A. Greene	
8.	A.	John Foss Insurance Co.	B.	New World Stove Co.	8. ____
	C.	14th Street Dress Shop	D.	Arthur Stein Paper Co.	
9.	A.	Gold Trucking Co.	B.	B. 8th Ave. Garage	9. ____
	C.	The First National Bank	D.	The Century Novelty Co.	
10.	A.	F. L. Doskow	B.	Natalie S. Doskow	10. ____
	C.	Samuel B. Doskow	D.	Arthur G. Doskor	

KEY (CORRECT ANSWERS)

1. A
2. B
3. D
4. D
5. D
6. A
7. C
8. B
9. C
10. B

TEST 4

DIRECTIONS: Each question from 1 through 10 consists of four names. For each question, choose the one of the four names that should be *LAST* if the four names were arranged in alphabetical order in accordance with the Rules for Alphabetical Filing given before. Read these rules carefully. Then, for each question, print in the space at the right the letter before the name that should be *LAST* in alphabetical order.

SAMPLE QUESTION

    A. Jane Earl   (2)
    B. James A. Earle   (4)
    C. James Earl   (1)
    D. J. Earle   (3)

The numbers in parentheses show the proper alphabetical order in which these names should be filed. Since the name that should be filed *LAST* is James A. Earle, the answer to the sample question is B.

1. A. Corral, Dr. Robert   B. Carrale, Prof. Robert
   C. Corren, R.   D. Corret, Ron

2. A. Rivera, Ilena   B. Riviera, Ilene
   C. Rivere, I.   D. Riviera Ice-Cream Co.

3. A. VonHogel, George   B. Volper, Gary
   C. Vonner, G.   D. Van Pefel, Gregory

4. A. David Kallish Stationery Co.
   B. Emerson Microfilm Company
   C. David Kalder Industrial Engineers Associated
   D. 5th Avenue Office Furniture Co.

5. A. A. Bennet, C.   B. Benett, Chuck
   C. Bennet, Chas.   D. Bennett, Charles

6. A. The Board of Higher Education
   B. National Education Commission
   C. Eakin, Hugh
   D. Nathan, Ellen

7. A. McCloud, I.   B. MacGowen, Ian
   C. McGowen, Arthur   D. Macale, Sean

8. A. Devine, Sarah   B. Devine, S.
   C. Devine, Sara H.   D. Devin, Sarah

9. A. Milstein, Louis   B. Milrad, Abraham P.
   C. Milstein, Herman   D. Milstien, Harold G.

10. A. Herfield, Lester L.   B. Herbstman, Nathan
    C. Henricksen, Ole A.   D. Herfeld, Burton G.

KEY (CORRECT ANSWERS)

1. D
2. B
3. C
4. A
5. D

6. B
7. C
8. A
9. D
10. A

TEST 5

DIRECTIONS: Same as for Test 4.

1. A. Francis Lattimore   B. H. Latham
   C. G. Lattimore   D. Hugh Latham   1.____

2. A. Thomas B. Morgan   B. B. Thomas Morgan
   C. T. Morgan   D. Thomas Bertram Morgan   2.____

3. A. Lawrence A. Villon   B. Chas. Valente
   C. Charles M. Valent   D. Lawrence De Villon   3.____

4. A. Alfred Devance   B. A. R. D'Amico
   C. Arnold De Vincent   D. A. De Pino   4.____

5. A. Dr. Milton A. Bergmann   B. Miss Evelyn M. Bergmenn
   C. Prof. E. N. Bergmenn   D. Mrs. L. B. Bergmann   5.____

6. A. George MacDougald   B. Thomas McHern
   C. William Macholt   D. Frank McHenry   6.____

7. A. Third National Bank B. Robt. Tempkin Corp.
   C. 32nd Street Carpet Co.   D. Wm. Templeton, Inc.   7.____

8. A. Mary Lobell Art Shop   B. John La Marca, Inc
   C. Lawyers' Guild   D. Frank Le Goff Studios   8.____

9. A. 9th Avenue Garage   B. Jos. Nuren Food Co.
   C. The New Book Store   D. Novelty Card Corp.   9.____

10. A. Murphy's Moving & Storage, Inc.   10.____
    B. Mid-Island Van Lines Corporation
    C. Mollone Bros. Moving & Storage, Inc.
    D. McShane Moving & Storage, Inc.

KEY (CORRECT ANSWERS)

1. C
2. D
3. A
4. C
5. B

6. B
7. C
8. A
9. B
10. A

TEST 6

DIRECTIONS: Each question contains four names numbered from 1 through 4 but not necessarily numbered in correct filing order. Answer each question by choosing the letter corresponding to the CORRECT filing order of the four names in accordance with the Rules for Alphabetic Filing given before. *PRINT THE LETTER OF THE CORRECT ANSWER IN THE SPACE AT THE RIGHT.*

SAMPLE QUESTION

1. Robert J. Smith
2. R. Jeffrey Smith
3. Dr. A. Smythe
4. Allen R. Smithers

A. 1, 2, 3, 4   B. 3, 1, 2, 4   C. 2, 1, 4, 3   D. 3, 2, 1, 4

Since the correct filing order, in accordance with the above rules, is 2, 1, 4, 3, the correct answer is C.

1.
   1. J. Chester VanClief
   2. John C. VanClief
   3. J. VanCleve
   4. Mary L. Vance

   A. 4, 3, 1, 2   B. 4, 3, 2, 1   C. 3, 1, 2, 4   D. 3, 4, 1, 2

   1.____

2.
   1. Community Development Agency
   2. Department of Social Services
   3. Board of Estimate
   4. Bureau of Gas and Electricity

   A. 3, 4, 1, 2   B. 1, 2, 4, 3   C. 2, 1, 3, 4   D. 1, 3, 4, 2

   2.____

3.
   1. Dr. Chas. K. Dahlman
   2. F. & A. Delivery Service
   3. Department of Water Supply
   4. Demano Men's Custom Tailors

   A. 1, 2, 3, 4   B. 1, 4, 2, 3   C. 4, 1, 2, 3   D. 4, 1, 3, 2

   3.____

4.
   1. 48th Street Theater
   2. Fourteenth Street Day Care Center
   3. Professor A. Cartwright
   4. Albert F. McCarthy

   A. 4, 2, 1, 3   B. 4, 3, 1, 2   C. 3, 2, 1, 4   D. 3, 1, 2, 4

   4.____

5.
   1. Frances D'Arcy
   2. Mario L. DelAmato
   3. William H. Diamond
   4. Robert J. DuBarry

   A. 1, 2, 4, 3   B. 2, 1, 3, 4   C. 1, 2, 3, 4   D. 2, 1, 3, 4

   5.____

6.
   1. Evelyn H. D'Amelio
   2. Jane R. Bailey
   3. Robert Bailey
   4. Frank Baily

   A. 1, 2, 3, 4   B. 1, 3, 2, 4   C. 2, 3, 4, 1   D. 3, 2, 4, 1

   6.____

7.
   1. Department of Markets
   2. Bureau of Handicapped Children
   3. Housing Authority Administration Building
   4. Board of Pharmacy

   7.____

| | A. | 2,1,3,4 | B. | 1,2,4,3 | C. | 1,2,3,4 | D. | 3,2,1,4 |

8. 1. William A. Shea Stadium
   2. Rapid Speed Taxi Co.
   3. Harry Stampler's Rotisserie
   4. Wilhelm Albert Shea

   A. 2, 3, 4, 1   B. 4, 1, 3, 2   C. 2, 4, 1, 3   D. 3, 4, 1, 2

9. 1. Robert S. Aaron, M. D.   2. Mrs. Norma S. Aaron
   3. Irving I. Aronson   4. Darius P. Aanonsen

   A. 1, 2, 3, 4   B. 2, 4, 1, 3   C. 4, 2, 3, 1   D. 4, 2, 1, 3

10. 1. The Gamut   2. Gilliar Drug Co., Inc.
    3. Georgette Cosmetology   4. Great Nock Pharmacy

    A. 1, 3, 2, 4   B. 3, 1, 4, 2   C. 1, 2, 3, 4   D. 1, 3, 4, 2

KEY (CORRECT ANSWERS)

1. A
2. D
3. B
4. D
5. C

6. D
7. D
8. C
9. D
10. A

TEST 7

DIRECTIONS: Each question consists of four names grouped vertically under four different filing arrangements lettered A, B, C, and D. In each question only one of the four arrangements lists the names in the correct filing order according to the Rules for Alphabetical Filing given before. Read these rules carefully. Then, for each question, select the correct filing arrangement, lettered A, B, C, or D and print in the space at the right the letter of that correct filing arrangement.

SAMPLE QUESTION

Arrangement A	*Arrangement B*	*Arrangement C*	*Arrangement D*
Arnold Robinson	Arthur Roberts	Arnold Robinson	Arthur Roberts
Arthur Roberts	J. B. Robin	Arthur Roberts	James Robin
J. B. Robin	James Robin	James Robin	J. B. Robin
James Robin	Arnold Robinson	J. B. Robin	Arnold Robinson

Since, in this sample, ARRANGEMENT B is the only one in which the four names are correctly arranged alphabetically, the answer is B.

1. *Arrangement A*
   Alice Thompson
   Arnold G. Thomas
   B. Thomas
   Eugene Thompkins
   Arrangement C
   B. Thomas Arnold
   G. Thomas
   Eugene Thompkins
   Alice Thompson

   Arrangement B
   Eugene Thompkins
   Alice Thompson
   Arnold G. Thomas
   B. Thomas
   Arrangement D
   Arnold G. Thomas
   B. Thomas
   Eugene Thompkins
   Alice Thompson

   1.____

2. *Arrangement A*
   Albert Green
   A. B. Green
   Frank E. Green
   Wm. Greenfield
   Arrangement C
   Albert Green
   Wm. Greenfield
   A. B. Green
   Frank E. Green

   Arrangement B
   A. B. Green
   Albert Green
   Frank E. Green
   Wm. Greenfield
   Arrangement D
   A. B. Green
   Frank E. Green
   Albert Green
   Wm. Greenfield

   2.____

3. *Arrangement A*
   Steven M. Comte
   Robt. Count
   Robert B. Count
   Steven Le Comte
   Arrangement C
   Steven M. Comte
   Steven Le Comte
   Robt. Count
   Robert B. Count

   Arrangement B
   Steven Le Comte
   Steven M. Comte
   Robert B. Count
   Robt. Count
   Arrangement D
   Robt. Count
   Robert B. Count
   Steven Le Comte
   Steven M. Comte

   3.____

4. *Arrangement A*   *Arrangement B*   4.____
   Prof. David Towner   Dr. Frank I. Tower
   Miss Edna Tower   Miss Edna Tower
   Dr. Frank I. Tower   Mrs. K. C. Towner
   Mrs. K. C. Towner   Prof. David Towner
   Arrangement C   *Arrangement D*
   Miss Edna Tower   Prof. David Towner
   Dr. Frank I. Tower   Mrs. K. C. Towner
   Prof. David Towner   Miss Edna Tower
   Mrs. K. C. Towner   Dr. Frank I. Tower

5. *Arrangement A*   *Arrangement B*   5.____
   The Jane Miller Shop   Joseph Millard Corp.
   Joseph Millard Corp.   The Jane Miller Shop
   John Muller & Co.   John Muller & Co.
   Jean Mullins, Inc.   Jean Mullins, Inc.
   Arrangement C   *Arrangement D*
   The Jane Miller Shop   Joseph Millard Corp.
   Jean Mullins, Inc.   John Muller & Co.
   John Muller & Co.   Jean Mullins, Inc.
   Joseph Millard Corp.   The Jane Miller Shop

6. *Arrangement A*   *Arrangement B*   6.____
   Anthony Delaney   Anthony Delaney
   A. M. D'Elia   A. De Landri
   A. De Landri   A. M. D'Elia
   Alfred De Monte   Alfred De Monte
   Arrangement C   *Arrangement D*
   A. De Landri   A. De Landri
   A. M. D'Elia   Anthony Delaney
   Alfred De Monte   A. M. D'Elia
   Anthony Delaney   Alfred De Monte

7. *Arrangement A*   *Arrangement B*   7.____
   D. McAllen   D. McAllen
   Lewis McBride   Doris MacAllister
   Doris MacAllister   Lewis McBride
   Lewis T. Mac Bride   Lewis T. MacBride
   Arrangement C   *Arrangement D*
   Doris MacAllister   Doris MacAllister
   Lewis T. MacBride   D. McAllen
   D. McAllen   Lewis T. MacBride
   Lewis McBride   Lewis McBride

8. *Arrangement A*
   6th Ave. Swim Shop
   The Sky Ski School
   Sport Shoe Store
   23rd Street Salon
   Arrangement C
   6th Ave. Swim Shop
   Sport Shoe Store
   The Sky Ski School
   23rd Street Salon

   Arrangement B
   23rd Street Salon
   The Sky Ski School
   6th Ave. Swim Shop
   Sport Shoe Store
   Arrangement D
   The Sky Ski School
   6th Ave. Swim Shop
   Sport Shoe Store
   23rd Street Salon

8._____

9. *Arrangement A*
   Charlotte Stair
   C. B. Stare
   Charles B. Stare
   Elaine La Stella
   Arrangement C
   Elaine La Stella
   Charlotte Stair
   C. B. Stare
   Charles B. Stare

   Arrangement B
   C. B. Stare
   Charles B. Stare
   Charlotte Stair
   Elaine La Stella
   Arrangement D
   Charles B. Stare
   C. B. Stare
   Charlotte Stair
   Elaine La Stella

9._____

10. *Arrangement A*
   John O'Farrell Corp.
   Finest Glass Co.
   George Fraser Co.
   4th Guarantee Bank
   Arrangement C
   John O'Farrell Corp.
   Finest Glass Co.
   4th Guarantee Bank
   George Fraser Co.

   Arrangement B
   Finest Glass Co.
   4th Guarantee Bank
   George Fraser Co.
   John O'Farrell Corp.
   Arrangement D
   Finest Glass Co.
   George Fraser Co.
   John O'Farrell Corp.
   4th Guarantee Bank

10._____

KEY (CORRECT ANSWERS)

1. D
2. B
3. A
4. C
5. B

6. D
7. C
8. A
9. C
10. B

TEST 8

DIRECTIONS: Same as for Test 7.

	Arrangement A	Arrangement B	Arrangement C	
1.	R. B. Stevens Chas. Stevenson Robert Stevens, Sr. Alfred T. Stevens	Alfred T. Stevens R. B. Stevens Robert Stevens, Sr. Chas. Stevenson	R. B. Stevens Robert Stevens, Sr. Alfred T. Stevens Chas. Stevenson	1.____
2.	Mr. A. T. Breen Dr. Otis C. Breen Amelia K. Brewington John Brewington	John Brewington Amelia K. Brewington Dr. Otis C. Breen Mr. A. T. Breen	Dr. Otis C. Breen Mr. A. T. Breen John Brewington Amelia K. Brewington	2.____
3.	J. Murphy J. J. Murphy John Murphy John J. Murphy	John Murphy John J. Murphy J. Murphy J. J. Murphy	J. Murphy John Murphy J. J. Murphy John J. Murphy	3.____
4.	Anthony DiBuono George Burns, Sr. Geo. T. Burns, Jr. Alan J. Byrnes	Geo. T. Burns, Jr. George Burns, Sr. Anthony DiBuono Alan J. Byrnes	George Burns, Sr. Geo. T. Burns, Jr. Alan J. Byrnes Anthony DiBuono	4.____
5.	James Macauley Frank A. McLowery Francis MacLaughry Bernard J. MacMahon	James Macauley Francis MacLoughry Bernard J. MacMahon Frank A. McLowery	Bernard J. MacMahon Francis MacLaughry Frank A. McLowery James Macauley	5.____
6.	A. J. DiBartolo, Sr. A. P. DiBartolo J. A. Bartolo Anthony J. Bartolo	J. A. Bartolo Anthony J. Bartolo A. P. DiBartolo A. J. DiBartolo, Sr.	Anthony J. Bartolo J. A. Bartolo A. J. DiBartolo, Sr. A. P. DiBartolo	6.____
7.	Edward Holmes Corp. Hillside Trust Corp Standard Insurance Co. The Industrial Surety Co.	Edward Holmes Corp. Hillside Trust Corp. The Industrial Surety Co. Standard Insurance Co.	Hillside Trust Corp. Edward Holmes Corp. The Industrial Surety Co. Standard Insurance Co.	7.____
8.	Cooperative Credit Co. Chas. Cooke Chemical Corp. John Fuller Baking Co. 4th Avenue Express Co.	Chas. Cooke Chemical Corp. Cooperative Credit Co. 4th Avenue Express Co. John Fuller Baking Co.	4th Avenue Express Co. John Fuller Baking Co. Chas. Cooke Chemical Corp. Cooperative Credit Co.	8.____

9. Mr. R. McDaniels   F. L. Ramsey   Robert Darling, Jr. Charles   9.____
    Robert Darling, Jr.   Mr. R. McDaniels   DeRhone
    F. L. Ramsey   Charles DeRhone   Mr. R. McDaniels
    Charles DeRhone   Robert Darling, Jr.   F. L. Ramsey

10. New York Omnibus Corp. John J. O'Brien Co.   Nova Scotia Canning Co.   10.____
    New York Shipping Co.   New York Omnibus Corp.   John J. O'Brien Co.
    Nova Scotia Canning Co. New York Shipping Co.   New York Omnibus Corp.
    John J. O'Brien Co.   Nova Scotia Caning Co.   New York Shipping Co.

KEY (CORRECT ANSWERS)

1. B
2. A
3. A
4. C
5. B

6. C
7. C
8. B
9. C
10. A

TEST 9

DIRECTIONS: Each question consists of a group of names. Consider each group of names as a unit. Determine in what position the name printed in *ITALICS* would be if the names in the group were *CORRECTLY* arranged in alphabetical order. If the name in *ITALICS* should be first, print the letter A; if second, print the letter B; if third, print the letter C; if fourth, print the letter D; and if fifth, print the letter E. *PRINT THE LETTER OF THE CORRECT ANSWER IN THE SPACE AT THE RIGHT.*

SAMPLE QUESTION

  J. W. Martin   2
  James E. Martin   4
  J. Martin   1
  George Martins   5
  James Martin   3

1. Albert Brown
   James Borenstein
   Frieda Albrecht
   Samuel Brown
   George Appelman

2. James Ryan
   Francis Ryan
   Wm. Roanan
   Frances S. Ryan
   Francis P. Ryan

3. Norman Fitzgibbons
   Charles F. Franklin
   Jas. Fitzgerald
   Andrew Fitzsimmons
   James P. Fitzgerald

4. Hugh F. Martenson
   A. S. Martinson
   Albert Martinsen
   Albert S. Martinson
   M. Martanson

5. Aaron M. Michelson
   Samuel Michels
   Arthur L. Michaelson, Sr.
   John Michell
   Daniel Michelsohn

1.____

2.____

3.____

4.____

5.____

6. *Chas. R. Connolly*   6.____
    Frank Conlon
    Charles S. Connolly
    Abraham Cohen
    Chas. Conolly

7. James McCormack   7.____
    Ruth MacNamara
    Kathryn McGillicuddy
    Frances Mason
    Arthur MacAdams

8. Dr. Francis Karell   8.____
    John Joseph Karelsen,
    Jr. John J.Karelsen,Sr.
    Mrs. Jeanette Kelly
    Estelle Karel

9. *The 5th Ave. Bus Co.*   9.____
    The Baltimore and Ohio Railroad
    3rd Ave. Elevated Co.
    Pennsylvania Railroad
    The 4th Ave. Trolley Line

10. Murray B. Cunitz   10.____
    Cunningham Duct Cleaning Corp.
    James A. Cunninghame
    Jason M. Cuomor
    Talmadge L. Cummings

KEY (CORRECT ANSWERS)

1. E
2. D
3. A
4. E
5. D

6. C
7. C
8. D
9. B
10. C

TEST 10

DIRECTIONS: A supervisor who is responsible for the proper maintenance and operation of the filing system in an office of a depart-ment should be able to instruct and guide his subordinates in the correct filing of office records. The following ques-tions,1 through 10, are designed to determine whether you can interpret and follow a prescribed filing procedure. These questions should be answered SOLELY on the basis of the fil-ing instructions which follow.

FILING INSTRUCTIONS FOR PERSONNEL DIVISION
DEPARTMENT X

The filing system of this division consists of three separate files, namely: (1) Employee File, (2) Subject File, (3) Correspondence File.

<u>Employee File</u>

This file contains a folder for each person currently employed in the department. Each report, memorandum, and letter which has been received from an official or employee of the department and which pertions to one employee only should be placed in the Employee File folder of the employee with whom the communication is concerned. (Note: This filing proce-dure also applies to a communication from a staff member who writes on a matter which con-cerns himself only.)

<u>Subject File</u>

Reports and memoranda originating in the department and dealing with personnel mat-ters affecting the entire staff or certain categories or groups of employees should be placed in the Subject File under the appropriate subject headings. The materials in this file are subdi-vided under the following five subject headings:

(1) Classification -- includes material on job analysis, change of title, reclassifica-tion of positions, etc.

(2) Employment -- includes material on appointment, promotion, re-instatement, and transfer.

(3) Health and Safety -- includes material dealing chiefly with the health and safety of employees.

(4) Staff Regulations -- includes material pertaining to rules and regulations gov-erning such working conditions as hours of work, lateness, vacation, leave of absence, etc.

(5) Training -- includes all material relating to employee training.

<u>Correspondence File</u>

All correspondence received from outside agencies, both public and private, and from persons outside the department, should be placed in the Correspondence File and cross ref-erenced as follows:

(1) When letters from outside agencies or persons relate to one or more employees currently employed in the department, a cross reference sheet should be placed in the Employee File folder of each employee mentioned.

(2) When letters from outside agencies or persons do not mention a specific employee or specific employees of the department, a cross reference sheet should be placed in the Subject File under the appropriate subject heading.

Questions 1-10 describe communications which have been received and acted upon by the Personnel Division of Department X, and which must be filed in accordance with the Filing Instructions for the Personnel Division.

The following filing operations may be performed in accordance with the above filing instructions:

- (A) Place in Employee File
- (B) Place in Subject File under Classification
- (C) Place in Subject File tinder Employment
- (D) Place in Subject File under Health and Safety
- (E) Place in Subject File under Staff Regulations
- (F) Place in Subject File under Training
- (G) Place in Correspondence File and cross reference in Employee File
- (H) Place in Correspondence File and cross reference in Subject File under Classification
- (I) Place in Correspondence File and cross reference in Subject File under Employment
- (J) Place in Correspondence File and cross reference in Subject File under Health and Safety
- (K) Place in Correspondence File and cross reference in Subject File under Staff Regulations
- (L) Place in Correspondence File and cross reference in Subject File under Training

DIRECTIONS: Examine each of questions 1 through 10 carefully. Then, in the space at the right, *print* the capital letter preceding the one of the filing operations listed above which MOST accurately carries out the Filing Instructions for the Personnel Division.

SAMPLE: A Clerk, Grade 2, in the department has sent in a memorandum requesting information regarding the amount of vacation due him.
The CORRECT answer is A.

1. Mr. Clark, a Clerk, Grade 5, has submitted an intradepartmental memorandum that the titles of all Clerks, Grade 5, in the department be changed to Administrative Assistant.   1.____

2. The secretary to the department has issued a staff order revising the schedule of Saturday work from a one-in-two to a one-in-four schedule.   2.____

3. The personnel officer of another agency has requested the printed transcripts of an in-service course recently conducted by the department.   3.____

4. Mary Smith, a secretary to one of the division chiefs, has sent in a request for a maternity leave of absence to begin on April 1 of this year and to terminate on March 31 of next year.   4.____

5. A letter has been received from a civic organization stating that they would like to know how many employees were promoted in the department during the last fiscal year.   5.____

6. The attorney for a municipal employees' organization has requested permission to represent Mr. James Roe, a departmental employee who is being brought up on charges of violating departmental regulations.   6.____

7. A letter has been received from Mr. Wright, a salesman for a paper company, who complains that Miss Jones, an information clerk in the department, has been rude and impertinent and has refused to give him information which should be available to the public.   7.____

8. Helen Brown, a graduate of Commercial High School, has sent a letter inquiring about an appointment as a provisional typist. 8.____

9. The National Office Managers' Society has sent a request to the department for information on its policies on tardiness and absenteeism. 9.____

10. A memorandum has been received from a division chief who states that employees in his unit have complained that their rest room is in a very unsanitary condition. 10.____

KEY (CORRECT ANSWERS)

1. B
2. E
3. L
4. A
5. I

6. G
7. G
8. I
9. K
10. D

FILING

EXAMINATION SECTION
TEST 1

DIRECTIONS: Questions 1 through 8 each show in Column I names written on four cards (lettered w, x, y, z) which have to be filed. You are to choose the option (lettered A, B, C, or D) in Column II which *BEST* represents the proper order of filing according to the Rules for Alphabetic Filing, given before, and the sample question given below. Print the letter of the correct answer in the space at the right.

SAMPLE QUESTION

	Column I		Column II
w.	Jane Earl	A.	w, y, z, x
x.	James A. Earle	B.	y, w, z, x
y.	James Earl	C.	x, y, w, z
z.	J. Earle	D.	x, w, y, z

The correct way to file the cards is:
- y. James Earl
- w. Jane Earl
- z. J. Earle
- x. James A. Earle

The correct filing order is shown by the letters, y, w, z, x (in that sequence). Since, in Column II, B appears in front of the letters, y, w, z, x (in that sequence), B is the correct answer to the sample question.

Now answer the following questions using that same procedure.

		Column I		Column II	
1.	w.	James Rothschild	A.	x, z, w, y	1.____
	x.	Julius B. Rothchild	B.	x, w, z, y	
	y.	B. Rothstein	C.	z, y, w, x	
	z.	Brian Joel Rothenstein	D.	z, w, x, y	
2.	w.	George S. Wise	A.	w, y, z, x	2.____
	x.	S. G. Wise	B.	x, w, y, z	
	y.	Geo. Stuart Wise	C.	y, x, w, z	
	z.	Prof. Diana Wise	D.	z, w, y, x	
3.	w.	10th Street Bus Terminal	A.	x, z, w, y	3.____
	x.	Buckingham Travel Agency	B.	y, x, w, z	
	y.	The Buckingham Theater	C.	w, z, y, x	
	z.	Burt Tompkins Studio	D.	x, w, y, z	
4.	w.	National Council of American Importers	A.	w, y, x, z	4.____
			B.	x, z, w, y	
	x.	National Chain Co. of Providence	C.	z, x, w, y	
	y.	National Council on Alcoholism	D.	z, x, y, w	
	z.	National Chain Co.			

5. w. Dr. Herbert Alvary   A. w, y, x, z   5._____
   x. Mr. Victor Alvarado   B. z, w, x, y
   y. Alvar Industries   C. y, z, x, w
   z. V. Alvarado   D. w, z, x, y

6. w. Joan MacBride   A. w, x, z, y   6._____
   x. Wm. Mackey   B. w, y, z, x
   y. Roslyn McKenzie   C. w, z, x, y
   z. Winifred Mackey   D. w, y, x, z

7. w. 3 Way Trucking Co.   A. y, x, z, w   7._____
   x. 3rd Street Bakery   B. y, z, w, x
   y. 380 Realty Corp.   C. x, y, z, w
   z. Three Lions Pub   D. x, y, w, z

8. w. Miss Rose Leonard   A. z, w, x, y   8._____
   x. Rev. Leonard Lucas   B. w, z, y, x
   y. Sylvia Leonard Linen Shop   C. w, x, z, y
   z. Rose S. Leonard   D. z, w, y, x

KEY (CORRECT ANSWERS)

1. A
2. D
3. B
4. D
5. C
6. A
7. C
8. B

TEST 2

DIRECTIONS: Questions 1 through 7 each show in Column I four names (lettered w, x, y, z) which have to be entered in an agency telephone directory. You are to choose the option (lettered A, B, C, or D) in Column II which *BEST* represents the proper order for entering them according to the Rules for Alphabetic Filing, given before, and the sample question given below.

SAMPLE QUESTION

    Column I   Column II
- w. Doris Jenkin   A. w, y, z, x
- x. Donald F. Jenkins   B. y, w, z, x
- y. Donald Jenkin   C. x, y, w, z
- z. D. Jenkins   D. x, w, y, z

The correct way to enter these names is:
- y. Donald Jenkin
- w. Doris Jenkin
- z. D. Jenkins
- x. Donald F. Jenkins

The correct order is shown by the letters y, w, z, x, in that sequence. Since, in Column II, B appears in front of the letters y, w, z, x, in that sequence, B is the correct answer to the sample question.

Now answer the following questions using the same procedure.

		Column I		Column II	
1.	w.	Lawrence Robertson	A.	x, y, w, z	1._____
	x.	Jack L. Robinson	B.	w, z, x, y	
	y.	John Robinson	C.	z, w, x, y	
	z.	William B. Roberson	D.	z, w, y, x	
2.	w.	P. N. Figueredo	A.	y, x, z, w	2._____
	x.	M. Alice Figueroa	B.	x, z, w, y	
	y.	Jose Figueredo	C.	x, w, z, y	
	z.	M. Alicia Figueroa	D.	y, w, x, z	
3.	w.	George Steven Keats	A.	y, x, w, z	3._____
	x.	George S. Keats	B.	z, y, x, w	
	y.	G. Samuel Keats	C.	x, z, w, y	
	z.	Dr. Samuel Keats	D.	w, z, x, y	
4.	w.	V. Merchant	A.	w, x, y, z	4._____
	x.	Dr. William Mercher	B.	w, y, z, x	
	y.	Prof. Victor Merchant	C.	z, y, w, x	
	z.	Dr. Walter Merchan	D.	z, w, y, x	
5.	w.	Brian McCoy	A.	z, x, y, w	5._____
	x.	William Coyne	B.	y, w, z, x	
	y.	Mr. William MacCoyle	C.	x, z, y, w	
	z.	Dr. D. V. Coyne	D.	w, y, z, x	

6.
- w. Ms. M. Rosie Buchanan
- x. Rosalyn M. Buchanan
- y. Rosie Maria Buchanan
- z. Rosa Marie Buchanan

A. z, y, x, w
B. w, z, x, y
C. w, z, y, x
D. z, x, y, w

6.____

7.
- w. Prof. Jonathan Praga
- x. Dr. Joan Prager
- y. Alan VanPrague
- z. Alexander Prague

A. w, z, y, x
B. w, x, z, y
C. x, w, z, y
D. x, w, y, z

7.____

KEY (CORRECT ANSWERS)

1. C
2. D
3. A
4. D
5. A
6. B
7. B

TEST 3

DIRECTIONS: Questions 1 through 10 each show in Column I names written on four cards (lettered w, x, y, z) which have to be filed. You are to choose the option (lettered A, B, C, or D) in Column II which *BEST* represents the proper order of filing according to the rules and sample question given below. The cards are to be filed according to the Rules for Alphabetical Filing, given before, and the sample question given below.

SAMPLE QUESTION

Column I		Column II
w. Jane Earl	A.	w, y, z, x
x. James A. Earle	B.	y, w, z, x
y. James Earl	C.	x, y, w, z
z. J. Earle	D.	x, w, y, z

The correct way to file the cards is:
- y. James Earl
- w. Jane Earl
- z. J. Earle
- x. James A. Earle

The correct filing order is shown by the letters y, w, z, x (in that order). Since, in Column II, B appears in front of the letters y, w, z, x (in that order), B is the correct answer to the sample question.

Now answer Questions 1 through 10 using the same procedure.

		Column I		Column II	
1.	w.	John Smith	A.	w, x, y, z	1.____
	x.	Joan Smythe	B.	y, z, x, w	
	y.	Gerald Schmidt	C.	y, z, w, x	
	z.	Gary Schmitt	D.	z, y, w, x	
2.	w.	A. Black	A.	w, x, y, z	2.____
	x.	Alan S. Black	B.	w, y, x, z	
	y.	Allan Black	C.	w, y, z, x	
	z.	Allen A. Black	D.	x, w, y, z	
3.	w.	Samuel Haynes	A.	w, x, y, z	3.____
	x.	Sam C. Haynes	B.	x, w, z, y	
	y.	David Haynes	C.	y, z, w, x	
	z.	Dave L. Haynes	D.	z, y, x, w	
4.	w.	Lisa B. McNeil	A.	x, y, w, z	4.____
	x.	Tom MacNeal	B.	x, z, y, w	
	y.	Lisa McNeil	C.	y, w, z, x	
	z.	Lorainne McNeal	D.	z, x, y, w	
5.	w.	Larry Richardson	A.	w, y, x, z	5.____
	x.	Leroy Richards	B.	y, x, z, w	
	y.	Larry S. Richards	C.	y, z, x, w	
	z.	Leroy C. Richards	D.	x, w, z, y	

6.
- w. Arlene Lane
- x. Arlene Cora Lane
- y. Arlene Clair Lane
- z. Arlene C. Lane

A. w, z, y, x
B. w, z, x, y
C. y, x, z, w
D. z, y, w, x

6.___

7.
- w. Betty Fish
- x. Prof. Ann Fish
- y. Norma Fisch
- z. Dr. Richard Fisch

A. w, x, z, y
B. x, w, y, z
C. y, z, x, w
D. z, y, w, x

7.___

8.
- w. Dr. Anthony David Lukak
- x. Mr. Steven Charles Lucas
- y. Mr. Anthony J. Lukak
- z. Prof. Steven C. Lucas

A. w, y, z, x
B. x, z, w, y
C. z, x, y, w
D. z, x, w, y

8.___

9.
- w. Martha Y. Lind
- x. Mary Beth Linden
- y. Martha W. Lind
- z. Mary Bertha Linden

A. w, y, z, x
B. w, y, x, z
C. y, w, z, x
D. y, w, x, z

9.___

10.
- w. Prof. Harry Michael MacPhelps
- x. Mr. Horace M. MacPherson
- y. Mr. Harold M. McPhelps
- z. Prof. Henry Martin MacPherson

A. w, z, x, y
B. w, y, z, x
C. z, x, w, y
D. x, z, y, w

10.___

KEY (CORRECT ANSWERS)

1. C
2. A
3. D
4. B
5. B
6. A
7. C
8. D
9. C
10. A

TEST 4

DIRECTIONS: Answer Questions 1 through 5 on the basis of the following information:

A certain shop keeps an informational card file on all suppliers and merchandise. On each card is the supplier's name, the contract number for the merchandise he supplies, and a delivery date for the merchandise. In this filing system, the supplier's name is filed alphabetically, the contract number for the merchandise is filed numerically, and the delivery date is filed chronologically.
In Questions 1 through 5 there are five notations numbered 1 through 5 shown in Column I. Each notation is made up of a supplier's name, a contract number, and a date which is to be filed according to the following rules:

    First: File in alphabetical order;
    Second: When two or more notations have the same supplier, file according to the contract number in numerical order beginning with the lowest number;
    Third: When two or more notations have the same supplier and contract number, file according to the date beginning with the earliest date.

In Column II the numbers 1 through 5 are arranged in four ways to show four different orders in which the merchandise information might be filed. Pick the answer (A., B, C, or D) in Column II in which the notations are arranged according to the above filing rules.

SAMPLE QUESTION

Column I	Column II
1. Cluney (4865) 6/17/02	A. 2, 3, 4, 1, 5
2. Roster (2466) 5/10/01	B. 2, 5, 1, 3, 4
3. Altool (7114) 10/15/02	C. 3, 2, 1, 4, 5
4. Cluney (5296) 12/18/01	D. 3, 5, 1, 4, 2
5. Cluney (4865) 4/8/02	

The correct way to file the cards is:
    3. Altool (7114) 10/15/02
    5. Cluney (4865) 4/8/02
    1. Cluney (4865) 6/17/02
    4. Cluney (5276) 12/18/01
    2. Roster (2466) 5/10/01

Since the correct filing order is 3, 5, 1, 4, 2, the answer to the sample question is D. Now answer Questions 1 through 5.

1.
Column I			Column II
1. warren	(96063)	3/30/03	A. 2, 4, 3, 5, 1
2. moore	(21237)	9/4/04	B. 2, 3, 5, 4, 1
3. newman	(10050)	12/12/03	C. 4, 5, 2, 3, 1
4. downs	(81251)	1/2/03	D. 4, 2, 3, 5, 1
5. oliver	(60145)	6/30/04	

1._____

2. 1. Henry   (40552) 7/6/04   A. 5, 4, 3, 1, 2   2.___
    2. Boyd   (91251) 9/1/03   B. 2, 3, 4, 1, 5
    3. George   (8196)   12/12/03   C. 2, 4, 3, 1, 5
    4. George   (31096) 1/12/04   D. 5, 2, 3, 1, 4
    5. West   (6109)   8/9/03

3. 1. Salba   (4670)   9/7/03   A. 5, 3, 1, 2, 4   3.___
    2. Salba   (51219) 3/1/03   B. 3, 1, 2, 4, 5
    3. Crete   (81562) 7/1/04   C. 3, 5, 4, 2, 1
    4. Salba   (51219) 1/11/04   D. 5, 3, 4, 2, 1
    5. Texi   (31549) 1/25/03

4. 1. Crayone   (87105) 6/10/04   A. 1, 2, 5, 3, 4   4.___
    2. Shamba   (49210) 1/5/03   B. 1, 5, 2, 3, 4
    3. Valiant   (3152)   5/1/04   C. 1, 5, 3, 4, 2
    4. Valiant   (3152)   1/9/04   D. 1, 5, 2, 4, 3
    5. Poro   (59613) 7/1/03

5. 1. Mackie   (42169) 12/20/03   A. 3, 2, 1, 5, 4   5.___
    2. Lebo   (5198)   9/12/02   B. 3, 2, 4, 5, 1
    3. Drummon   (99631) 9/9/04   C. 3, 5, 2, 4, 1
    4. Lebo   (15311) 1/25/02   D. 3, 5, 4, 2, 1
    5. Harvin   (81765) 6/2/03

KEY (CORRECT ANSWERS)

1. D
2. B
3. B
4. D
5. C

TEST 5

DIRECTIONS: Each of Questions 1 through 8 represents five cards to be filed, numbered 1 through 5 in Column I. Each card is made up of the employee's name, the date of a work assignment, and the work assignment code number shown in parentheses. The cards are to be filed according to the following rules:

First: File in alphabetical order;
Second: When two or more cards have the same employee's name, file according to the assignment date beginning with the earliest date;
Third: When two or more cards have the same employee's name and the same date, file according to the work assignment number beginning with the lowest number.

Column II shows the cards arranged in four different orders. Pick the answer (A, B, C, or D) in Column II which shows the cards arranged correctly according to the above filing rules.

SAMPLE QUESTION

Column I
1. Cluney 4/8/02 (486503)
2. Roster 5/10/01 (246611)
3. Altool 10/15/02 (711433)
4. Cluney 12/18/02 (527610)
5. Cluney 4/8/02 (486500)

Column II
A. 2, 3, 4, 1, 5
B. 2, 5, 1, 3, 4
C. 3, 2, 1, 4, 5
D. 3, 5, 1, 4, 2

The correct way to file the cards is:
3. Altool 10/15/02 (711433)
5. Cluney 4/8/02 (486500)
1. Cluney 4/8/02 (486503)
4. Cluney 12/18/02 (527610)
2. Roster 5/10/01 (246611)

The correct filing order is shown by the numbers in front of each name (3, 5, 1, 4, 2). The answer to the sample question is the letter in Column II in front of the numbers 3, 5, 1, 4, 2. This answer is D.

Now answer Questions 1 through 8 according to these rules.

1.
   1. Kohls   4/2/02   (125677)
   2. Keller   3/21/02   (129698)
   3. Jackson   4/10/02   (213541)
   4. Richards 1/9/03   (347236)
   5. Richmond 12/11/01 (379321)

   A. 1, 2, 3, 4, 5
   B. 3, 2, 1, 4, 5
   C. 3, 1, 2, 4, 5
   D. 5, 2, 1, 3, 4

2.
   1. Burroughs 5/27/02   (237896)
   2. Charlson 1/16/02   (114537)
   3. Carlsen   12/2/02   (114377)
   4. Burton   5/1/02   (227096)
   5. Charlson 12/2/02   (114357)

   A. 1, 4, 3, 2, 5
   B. 4, 1, 5, 3, 2
   C. 1, 4, 3, 5, 2
   D. 4, 1, 3, 5, 2

3. A. Ungerer 11/11/02 (537924)   A. 1, 5, 3, 2, 4   3.__
    B. Winters   1/10/02   (657834)   B. 5, 1, 3, 4, 2
    C. Ventura   12/1/02   (698694)   C. 3, 5, 1, 2, 4
    D. Winters   10/11/02 (675654)   D. 1, 5, 3, 4, 2
    E. Ungaro   1/10/02   (684325)

4. 1. Norton   3/12/03   (071605)   A. 1, 4, 2, 3, 5   4.__
    2. Morris   2/26/03   (068931)   B. 3, 5, 2, 4, 1
    3. Morse   5/12/03   (142358)   C. 2, 4, 3, 5, 1
    4. Morris   2/26/03   (068391)   D. 4, 2, 5, 3, 1
    5. Morse   2/26/03   (068391)

5. 1. Eger   4/19/02   (874129)   A. 3, 4, 1, 2, 5   5.__
    2. Eihler   5/19/03   (875329)   B. 1, 4, 5, 2, 3
    3. Ehrlich 11/19/02 (874839)   C. 4, 1, 3, 2, 5
    4. Eger   4/19/02   (876129)   D. 1, 4, 3, 5, 2
    5. Eihler   5/19/02   (874239)

6. 1. Johnson 12/21/02 (786814)   A. 2, 4, 3, 5, 1   6.__
    2. Johns   12/21/03 (801024)   B. 4, 2, 5, 3, 1
    3. Johnson 12/12/03 (762814)   C. 4, 5, 3, 1, 2
    4. Jackson 12/12/03 (862934)   D. 5, 3, 1, 2, 4
    5. Johnson 12/12/03 (762184)

7. 1. Fuller   7/12/02   (598310)   A. 2, 1, 5, 4, 3   7.__
    2. Fuller   7/2/02   (598301)   B. 1, 2, 4, 5, 3
    3. Fuller   7/22/02   (598410)   C. 1, 4, 5, 2, 3
    4. Fuller   7/17/03   (598710)   D. 2, 1, 3, 5, 4
    5. Fuller   7/17/03   (598701)

8. 1. Perrine 10/27/99 (637096)   A. 3, 4, 5, 1, 2   8.__
    2. Perrone 11/14/02 (767609)   B. 3, 2, 5, 4, 1
    3. Perrault 10/15/98 (629706)   C. 5, 3, 4, 1, 2
    4. Perrine 10/17/02 (373656)   D. 4, 5, 1, 2, 3
    5. Perine   10/17/01 (376356)

KEY (CORRECT ANSWERS)

1. B
2. A
3. B
4. D
5. D
6. B
7. D
8. C

TEST 6

DIRECTIONS: Each question or incomplete statement is followed by several suggested answers or completions. Select the one that BEST answers the question or completes the statement. PRINT THE LETTER OF THE CORRECT ANSWER IN THE SPACE AT THE RIGHT.

1. Which one of the following BEST describes the usual arrangement of a tickler file?   1._____

   A. Alphabetical B. Chronological
   C. Numerical   D. Geographical

2. Which one of the following is the LEAST desirable filing practice?   2._____

   A. Using staples to keep papers together
   B. Filing all material without regard to date
   C. Keeping a record of all materials removed from the files
   D. Writing filing instructions on each paper prior to filing

3. The one of the following records which it would be MOST advisable to keep in alphabetical order is a   3._____

   A. continuous listing of phone messages, including time and caller, for your supervisor
   B. listing of individuals currently employed by your agency in a particular title
   C. record of purchases paid for by the petty cash fund
   D. dated record of employees who have borrowed material from the files in your office

4. Tickler systems are used in many legal offices for scheduling and calendar control. Of the following, the LEAST common use of a tickler system is to   4._____

   A. keep papers filed in such a way that they may easily be retrieved
   B. arrange for the appearance of witnesses when they will be needed
   C. remind lawyers when certain papers are due
   D. arrange for the gathering of certain types of evidence

5. A type of file which permits the operator to remain seated while the file can be moved backward and forward as required is BEST termed a   5._____

   A. lateral file   B. movable file
   C. reciprocating file   D. rotary file

6. In which of the following cases would it be MOST desirable to have two cards for one individual in a single alphabetic file? The individual has   6._____

   A. a hyphenated surname
   B. two middle names
   C. a first name with an unusual spelling
   D. a compound first name

KEY (CORRECT ANSWERS)

1. B
2. B
3. B
4. A
5. C
6. A

FILING

EXAMINATION SECTION
TEST 1

Question 1-9

DIRECTIONS: An important part of the duties of an office worker in a public agency is to file office records. Questions 1 to 9 are designed to determine whether you can file records correctly. Each of these questions consists of four names. For each question, select the one of the four names that should be *FOURTH* if the four names were arranged in alphabetical order. *PRINT THE LETTER OF THE CORRECT ANSWER IN THE SPACE AT THE RIGHT.*

1. A. 6th National Bank   B. Sexton Lock Co.   1.____
    C. The 69th Street League   D. Thomas Saxon Corp,

2. A. 4th Avenue Printing Co.   B. The Four Corners Corp.   2.____
    C. Dr. Milton Fournet   D. The Martin Fountaine Co.

3. A. Mr. Chas. Le Mond   B. Model Express, Inc.   3.____
    C. Lenox Enterprises   D. Mobile Supply Co.

4. A. Frank Waller Johnson   B. Frank Walter Johnson   4.____
    C. Wilson Johnson   D. Frank W. Johnson

5. A. Miss Anne M. Carlsen   B. Mrs, Albert S. Carlson   5.____
    C. Mr. Alan Ross Carlsen   D. Dr. Anthony Ash Carlson

6. A. Delware Paper Co.   B. William Del Ville   6.____
    C. Ralph A. Delmar   D. Wm. K. Del Ville

7. A. The Lloyd Disney Co.   B. Mrs. Raymond Norris   7.____
    C. Oklahoma Envelope, Inc.   D. Miss Esther O'Neill

8. A. The Olympic Eraser Co.   B. Mrs. Raymond Norris   8.____
    C. Oklahoma Envelope, Inc.   D. Miss Esther O'Neill

9. A. Patricia MacNamara   B. Eleanor McNally   9.____
    C. Robt. MacPherson, Jr.   D. Helen McNair

Questions 10 - 21

DIRECTIONS: Questions 10 through 21 are to be answered on the basis of the usual rules for alphabetical filing. For each question, indicate in the space at the right the letter preceding the name which should be *THIRD* in alphabetical order.

10. A. Russell Cohen   B. Henry Cohn   10.____
    C. Wesley Chambers   D. Arthur Connors

11. A. Wanda Jenkins   B. Pauline Jennings   11.____
    C. Leslie Jantzenberg   D. Rudy Jensen

12. A. Arnold Wilson   B. Carlton Willson   12.____
    C. Duncan Williamson   D. Ezra Wilston

13. A. Joseph M. Buchman   B. Gustave Bozzerman   13.____
    C. Constantino Brunelli D. Armando Buccino

14. A. Barbara Waverly   B. Corinne Warterdam   14.____
    C. Dennis Waterman   D. Harold Wartman

15. A. Jose Mejia   B. Bernard Mendelsohn   15.____
    C. Antonio Mejias   D. Richard Mazzitelli

16. A. Hesselberg, Norman J. B. Hesselman, Nathan B.   16.____
    C. Hazel, Robert S.   D. Heintz, August J.

17. A. Oshins, Jerome   B. Ohsie, Marjorie   17.____
    C. O'Shaugn, F.J.   D. O'Shea, Frances

18. A. Petrie, Joshua A.   B. Pendleton, Oscar   18.____
    C. Pertwee, Joshua   D. Perkins, Warren G.

19. A. Morganstern, Alfred   B. Morganstern, Albert   19.____
    C. Monroe, Mildred   D. Modesti, Ernest

20. A. More, Stewart   B. Moorhead, Jay   20.____
    C. Moore, Benjamin   D. Moffat, Edith

21. A. Ramirez, Paul   B. Revere, Pauline   21.____
    C. Ramos, Felix   D. Ramazotti, Angelo

KEY (CORRECT ANSWERS)

1. C   11. B
2. A   12. A
3. B   13. D
4. B   14. C
5. D   15. C

6. A   16. A
7. C   17. D
8. D   18. C
9. B   19. B
10. B   20. B

21. C

TEST 2

DIRECTIONS: Each question or incomplete statement is followed by several suggested answers or completions. Select the one that BEST answers the question or completes the statement. *PRINT THE LETTER OF THE CORRECT ANSWER IN THE SPACE AT THE RIGHT.*

Questions 1 - 4

DIRECTIONS: Answer Questions 1 through 4 on the basis of the following alphabetical rules.

RULES FOR ALPHABETICAL FILING

Names of Individuals

The names of individuals are filed in strict alphabetical order, *first* according to the last name, *then* according to first name or initial, and *finally* according to middle name or initial. For example: George Allen precedes Edward Bell and Leonard Reston precedes Lucille Reston.

When last names are the same, for example, A. Green and Agnes Green, the one with the initial comes before the one with the name written out when the first initials are identical,

Prefixes such as De, O', Mac, Mc, and Van are filed as written and are treated as part of the names to which they are connected. For example: Gladys McTeaque is filed before Frances Meadows.

1. If the following four names were put into an alphabetical list, what would the *FIRST* name on the list be?

    A. Wm. C. Paul
    B. W. Paul
    C. Alice Paul
    D. Alyce Paule

1.____

2. If the following four names were put into an alphabetical list *what* would the *THIRD* name on the list be?

    A. I. MacCarthy
    B. Irene MacKarthy
    C. Ida McCaren
    D. I. A. McCarthy

2.____

3. If the following four names were put into an alphabetical list, *what* would the *SECOND* name on the list be?

    A. John Gilhooley
    B. Ramon Gonzalez
    C. Gerald Gilholy
    D. Samuel Gilvecchio

3.____

4. If the following four names were put into an alphabetical list, *what,* would the *FOURTH name* on the list be?

    A. Michael Edwinn
    B. James Edwards
    C. Mary Edwin
    D. Carlo Edwards

4.____

Questions 5-9

DIRECTIONS: Questions 5 to 9 consist of a group of names which are to be arranged in alphabetical order for filing.

5. Of the following, the name which should be filed FIRST is 5.____

   A. Joseph J. Meadeen   B. Gerard L. Meader
   C. John F. Madcar   D. Philip F. Malder

6. Of the following, the name which should be filed LAST is 6.____

   A. Stephen Fischer   B. Benjamin Fitchmann
   C. Thomas Fishman   D. Augustus S. Fisher

7. The name which should be filed SECOND is 7.____

   A. Yeatman, Frances   B. Yeaton, C.S.
   C. Yeatman, R.M.   D. Yeats, John

8. The name which should be filed THIRD is 8.____

   A. Hauser, Ann   B. Hauptmann, Jane
   C. Hauster, Mary   D. Rauprich, Julia

9. The name which should be filed SECOND is 9.____

   A. Flora McDougall   B. Fred E. MacDowell
   C. Juanita Mendez   D. James A. Madden

Questions 10-14

DIRECTIONS: Answer questions 10 through 14 based on an alphabetical arrangement of the following list of names.

Walker, Carol J.	Wacht, Michael	Wade, Ethel
Wall, Fredrick	Wall, Francis	Wall, Frank
Wachs, Paul	Walker, Carol L.	Wagner, Arthur
Walters, Daniel	Wade, Ellen	Wald, William
Wagner, Allen	Walters, David	Walker, Carmen

10. The 4th name on the alphabetized list would be 10.____

    A. Wade, Ellen   B. Wade, Ethel
    C. Wagner, Allen   D. Wagner, Arthur

11. The 7th name on the alphabetized list would be 11.____

    A. Walker, Carmen   B. Walker, Carol J.
    C. Walker, Carol L.   D. Wald, William

12. The name that would come immediately AFTER Wagner, Arthur on the alphabetized list would be 12.____

    A. Wade, Ethel   B. Wagner, Allen
    C. Wald, William   D. Walker, Carol L.

13. The name that would come immediately BEFORE Wall, Frank would be 13.____

    A. Wall, Francis   B. Wall, Fredrick
    C. Walters, David   D. Walters, Daniel

14. The 12th name on the alphabetized list would be 14.____

    A. Walker, Carol L. B. Wald, William
    C. Wall, Francis D. Wall, Frank

KEY (CORRECT ANSWERS)

1. C
2. C
3. A
4. A
5. C

6. B
7. C
8. A
9. D
10. B

11. D
12. C
13. A
14. D

TEST 3

DIRECTIONS: Each question or incomplete statement is followed by several suggested answers or completions. Select the one that *BEST* answers the question or completes the statement. *PRINT THE LETTER OF THE CORRECT ANSWER IN THE SPACE AT THE RIGHT.*

Questions 1-8

DIRECTIONS: Questions 1 through 8 are based on the Rules of Alphabetical Filing given below. Read these rules carefully before answering the questions.

Names of People
1. The names of people are filed in strict alphabetical order, first according to the last name, then according to first name or initial, and finally according to middle name or initial. For example: George Allen comes before Edward Bell, and Leonard P. Reston comes before Lucille B. Reston.

2. When last names are the same, for example, A. Green and Agnes Green, the one with the initial comes before the one with the name written out when the first initials are identical.

3. When first and last names are alike and the middle name is given, for example, John David Doe and John Devoe Doe, the names should be filed in alphabetical order of the middle names.

4. When first and last names are the same, a name without a middle initial comes before one with a middle name or initial. For example: John Doe comes before John A. Doe and John Alan Doe.

5. When first and last names are the same, a name with a middle initial comes before one with a middle name beginning with the same initial. For example: Jack R. Hertz comes before Jack Richard Hertz.

6. Prefixes such De, O', Mac, Mc and Van are filed as written and are treated as part of the names to which they are connected. For example: Robert O'Dea is filed before David Olsen.

7. Abbreviated names are treated as if they were spelled out. For example: Chas. is filed as Charles and Thos. is filed as Thomas.

8. Titles and designations such as Dr., Mr., and Prof, are disregarded in filing.

Names of Organizations

1. The names of business organizations are filed according to the order in which each word in the name appears. When an organization name bears the name of a person, it is filed according to the rules for filing names of people as given above. For example: William Smith Service Co. comes before Television Distributors, Inc.

2. Where bureau, board, office or department appears as the first part of the title of a governmental agency, that agency should be filed under the word in the title expressing the chief function of the agency. For example: Bureau of Budget would be filed as if written Budget, (Bureau of the). The Department of Personnel would be filed as if written Personnel, (Department of).

3. When the following words are part of an organization, they are disregarded: the, of, and.

4. When there are numbers in a name, they are treated as if they were spelled out. For example: 10th Street Bootery is filed as Tenth Street Bootery.

Each question from 1 through 8 contains four names numbered from 1 through 4 but not necessarily numbered in correct filing order. Answer each question by choosing the letter corresponding to the CORRECT filing order of the four names in accordance with the above rules.

Sample question:

  1. Robert J. Smith
  2. R. Jeffrey Smith
  3. Dr. A. Smythe
  4. Allen R. Smithers

A. 1, 2, 3, 4 B. 3, 1, 2, 4 C. 2, 1, 4, 3 D. 3, 2, 1, 4

Since the correct filing order, in accordance with the above rules, is 2, 1, 4, 3, the correct answer is C.

1. 1. J. Chester VanClief 2. John C. VanClief
  3. J. VanCleve   4. Mary L. Vance

 A. 4, 3, 1, 2 B. 4, 3, 2, 1 C. 3, 1, 2, 4 D. 3, 4, 1, 2

2. 1. Community Development Agency
  2. Department of Social Services
  3. Board of Estimate
  4. Bureau of Gas and Electricity

 A. 3, 4, 1, 2 B. 1, 2, 4, 3 C. 2, 1, 3, 4 D. 1, 3, 4, 2

3. 1. Dr. Chas. K. Dahlman
  2. F. & A. Delivery Service
  3. Department of Water Supply
  4. Demano Men's Custom Tailors

 A. 1, 2, 3, 4 B. 1, 4, 2, 3 C. 4, 1, 2, 3 D. 4, 1, 3, 2

4. 1. 48th Street Theater
  2. Fourteenth Street Day Care Center
  3. Professor A. Cartwright
  4. Albert F. McCarthy

 A. 4, 2, 1, 3 B. 4, 3, 1, 2 C. 3, 2, 1, 4 D. 3, 1, 2, 4

5. 1. Frances D'Arcy 2. Mario L. DelAmato
    3. William R. Diamond 4. Robert J. DuBarry

    A. 1, 2, 4, 3   B. 2, 1, 3, 4   C. 1, 2, 3, 4   D. 2, 1, 3, 4

    5.___

6. 1. Evelyn H. D'Amelio 2. Jane R. Bailey
    3. Robert Bailey 4. Frank Baily

    A. 1, 2, 3, 4   B. 1, 3, 2, 4   C. 2, 3, 4, 1   D. 3, 2, 4, 1

    6.___

7. 1. Department of Markets
    2. Bureau of Handicapped Children
    3. Housing Authority Administration Building
    4. Board of Pharmacy

    A. 2, 1, 3, 4   B. 1, 2, 4, 3   C. 1, 2, 3, 4   D. 3, 2, 1, 4

    7.___

8. 1. William A. Shea Stadium
    2. Rapid Speed Taxi Co.
    3. Harry Stampler's Rotisserie
    4. Wilhelm Albert Shea

    A. 2, 3, 4, 1   B. 4, 1, 3, 2   C. 2, 4, 1, 3   D. 3, 4, 1, 2

    8.___

Questions 9-18.

DIRECTIONS: Questions 9 through 18 each show in Column I names written on four ledger cards (lettered w, x, y, z) which have to be filed. You are to choose the option (lettered A, B, C, or D) in Column II which *BEST* represents the proper order for filing the cards.

SAMPLE

Column I
w. John Stevens
x. John D. Stevenson
y. Joan Stevens
z. J. Stevenson

Column II
A. w, y, z, x
B. y, w, z, x
C. x, y, w, z
D. x, w, y, z

The correct way to file the cards is:
y. Joan Stevens
w. John Stevens
z. J. Stevenson
x. John D. Stevenson

The correct order is shown by the letters y, w, z, x in that sequence. Since, in Column II, B appears in front of the letters y, w, z, x in that sequence, B is the correct answer to the sample question.

Now, answer the following questions, using the same procedure.

9. Column I
    w. Juan Montoya
    x. Manuel Montenegro
    y. Victor Matos
    z. Victoria Maltos

    Column II
    A. y, z, x, w
    B. z, y, x, w
    C. z, y, w, x
    D. y, x, z, w

4 (#3)

10.
- w. Frank Carlson
- x. Robert Carlton
- y. George Carlson
- z. Frank Carlton

A. z, x, w, y
B. z, y, x, w
C. w, y, z, x
D. w, z, y, x

11.
- w. Carmine Rivera
- x. Jose Rivera
- y. Frank River
- z. Joan Rivers

A. y, w, x, z
B. y, x, w, z
C. w, x, y, z
D. w, x, z, y

12.
- w. Jerome Mathews
- x. Scott A. Matthew
- y. Charles B. Matthew
- z. Scott C. Mathews

A. w, y, z, x
B. z, y, x, w
C. z, w, x, y
D. w, z, y, x

13.
- w. John McMahan
- x. John P. MacMahan
- y. Joseph DeMayo
- z. Joseph D. Mayo

A. w, x, y, z
B. y, x, z, w
C. x, w, y, z
D. y, x, w, z

14.
- w. Raymond Martinez
- x. Ramon Martinez
- y. Prof. Ray Martinez
- z. Dr. Raymond Martin

A. z, x, y, w
B. z, y, x, w
C. z, w, y, x
D. y, x, w, z

15.
- w. Mr. Robert Vincent Mackintosh
- x. Robert Reginald Macintosh
- y. Roger V. McIntosh
- z. Robert R. Mackintosh

A. y, x, z, w
B. x, w, z, y
C. x, w, y, z
D. x, z, w, y

16.
- w. Dr. D. V. Facsone
- x. Prof. David Fascone
- y. Donald Facsone
- z. Mrs. D. Fascone

A. y, w, z, x
B. w, y, x, z
C. w, y, z, x
D. z, w, x, y

17.
- w. Johnathan Q. Addams
- x. John Quincy Adams
- y. J. Quincy Addams
- z. Jerimiah Adams

A. z, x, w, y
B. z, x, y, w
C. y, w, x, z
D. x, w, z, y

18.
- w. Nehimiah Persoff
- x. Newton Pershing
- y. Newman Perring
- z. Nelson Persons

A. w, z, x, y
B. x, z, y, w
C. y, x, w, z
D. z, y, w, x

KEY (CORRECT ANSWERS)

1. A
2. D
3. B
4. D
5. C

6. D
7. D
8. C
9. B
10. C

11. A
12. D
13. B
14. A
15. D

16. C
17. B
18. C

TEST 4

Questions: 1 - 13

DIRECTIONS: Each question from 1 through 13 contains four names. For each question, choose the name that should be FIRST if the four names are to be arranged in alphabetical order in accordance with the Rule for Alphabetical Filing of Names of People given below. Read this rule carefully. Then, for each question, mark your answer space with the letter that is next to the name that should be first in alphabetical order.

RULE FOR ALPHABETICAL FILING OF NAMES OF PEOPLE

The names of people are filed in strict alphabetical order, first according to the last name, then according to the first name. For example: George Allen comes before Edward Bell, and Alice Reston comes before Lucille Reston.

SAMPLE QUESTION
A. Roger Smith (2)
B. Joan Smythe (4)
C. Alan Smith (1)
D. James Smithe (3)

The numbers in parentheses show the proper alphabetical order in which these names should be filed. Since the name that should be filed *first* is Alan Smith, the correct answer to the sample question is C.

1. A. William Claremont   B. Antonio Clements
   C. Anthony Clemente   D. William Claymont

2. A. Wayne Fumando   B. Sarah Femando
   C. Susan Fumando   D. Wilson Femando

3. A. Wilbur Hanson   B. Wm. Hansen
   C. Robert Hansen   D. Thomas Hanson

4. A. George St. John   B. Thomas Santos
   C. Frances Starks   D. Mary S. Stranum

5. A. Franklin Carrol   B. Timothy Carrol
   C. Timothy S. Carol   D. Frank F. Carroll

6. A. Christie-Barry Storage   B. John Christie-Barry
   C. The Christie-Barry Company   D. Anne Christie-Barrie

7. A. Inter State Travel Co.   B. Interstate Car Rental
   C. Inter State Trucking   D. Interstate Lending Inst.

8. A. The Los Angeles Tile Co.   B. Anita F. Los
   C. The Lost & Found Detective Agency   D. Jason Los-Brio

9. A. Prince Charles   B. Prince Charles Coiffures
   C. Chas. F. Prince   D. Thomas A. Charles

10. A. U.S. Dept. of Agriculture   B. United States Aircraft Co.   10._____
    C. U.S. Air Transport, Inc.   D. The United Union

11. A. Meyer's Art Shop   B. Frank B. Meyer   11._____
    C. Meyers' Paint Store   D. Meyer and Goldberg

12. A. David Des Laurier   B. Des Moines Flower Shop   12._____
    C. Henry Desanto   D. Mary L. Desta

13. A. Jeffrey Van Der Meer   B. Jeffrey M. Vander   13._____
    C. Jeffrey Van   D. Wallace Meer

KEY (CORRECT ANSWERS)

1. A   6. D
2. B   7. B
3. C   8. B
4. A   9. D
5. C   10. C

11. A
12. C
13. D

TEST 5

Questions: 1-10

DIRECTIONS: Questions 1 to 10 are to be answered on the basis of the usual rules of filing. Column I lists, next to the numbers 1 to 10, the names of 10 clinic patients. Column II lists, next to the letters A to D, the headings of file drawers into which you are to place the records of these patients. For each question, indicate in the space at the right the letter preceding the heading of the file drawer in which the record should be filed.

COLUMN I

1. Charles Coughlin
2. Mary Carstairs
3. Joseph Collin
4. Thomas Chelsey
5. Cedric Chalmers
6. Mae Clarke
7. Dora Copperhead
8. Arnold Cohn
9. Charlotte Crumboldt
10. Frances Celine

COLUMN II

A. Cab-Cep
B. Ceq-Cho
C. Chr-Coj
D. Cok-Czy

1._____
2._____
3._____
4._____
5._____
6._____
7._____
8._____
9._____
10._____

Questions 11-18

DIRECTIONS: Questions 11 to 18 are to be answered on the basis of the usual rules of filing. Column I lists, next to the numbers 11 to 18, the names of 8 clinic patients. Column II lists, next to the letters A to O, the headings of file drawers into which you are to place the records of these patients. For each question, indicate in the space at the right the letter preceding the heading of the file drawer in which the record should be filed.

COLUMN I

11. Thomas Adams
12. Joseph Albert
13. Frank Anaster
14. Charles Abt
15. John Alfred
16. Louis Aron
17. Francis Amos
18. William Adler

COLUMN II

A. Aab-Abi	I. Akp-Ald		11._____
B. Abj-Ach	J. Ale-Amo		12._____
C. Aci-Aco	K. Amp-Aor		13._____
D. Acp-Ada	L. Aos-Apr		14._____
E. Adb-Afr	M. Aps-Asi		15._____
F. Afs-Ago	N. Asj-Ati		16._____
G. Agp-Ahz	O. Atj-Awz		17._____
H. Aia-Ako			18._____

Questions: 19 - 28

DIRECTIONS: Questions 19 through 28 are to be answered on the basis of the usual rules of filing. Column I lists, next to the numbers 19 through 28, the names of 10 clinic patients. Column II lists, next to the letters A to D the headings of file drawers into which you are to place the medical records of these patients. For each question, indicate in the space at the right the letter preceding the heading of the file drawer in which the record should be filed.

COLUMN I		COLUMN II		
19.	Frank Shea	A.	Sab-Sej	19.___
20.	Rose Seaborn	B.	Sek-Sio	20.___
21.	Samuel Smollin	C.	Sip-Soo	21.___
22.	Thomas Shur	D.	Sop-Syz	22.___
23.	Ben Schaefer			23.___
24.	Shirley Strauss			24.___
25.	Harry Spiro			25.___
26.	Dora Skelly			26.___
27.	Sylvia Smith			27.___
28.	Arnold Selz			28.___

KEY (CORRECT ANSWERS)

1.	D	16.	M
2.	A	17.	J
3.	D	18.	E
4.	B	19.	B
5.	B	20.	A
6.	C	21.	C
7.	D	22.	B
8.	C	23.	A
9.	D	24.	D
10.	A	25.	D
11.	D	26.	C
12.	I	27.	C
13.	K	28.	B
14.	B		
15.	J		

EXAMINATION SECTION
TEST 1

DIRECTIONS: Each question or incomplete statement is followed by several suggested answers or completions. Select the one that *BEST* answers the question or completes the statement. *PRINT THE LETTER OF THE CORRECT ANSWER IN THE SPACE AT THE RIGHT.*

1. The MOST important characteristic of a tickler card file is that the cards are arranged according to

    A. subject matter
    B. the date on which action is to be taken
    C. the name of the individual on the card
    D. the order of importance of the items contained on the cards

    1.____

2. As a clerk in a city department, one of your duties is to maintain the files in your bureau. Material from these files is sometimes used by other bureaus. You frequently find that you are unable to locate some material because it has been removed from the files and is evidently being used by some other bureau. The BEST way to correct this situation is to

    A. have an out-of-file card filled out and filed when ever material is borrowed from the files
    B. forbid employees of other bureaus to borrow material from the files unless they promise to return it promptly
    C. provide other bureaus with duplicate files
    D. notify your supervisor whenever an employee from another bureau is slow in returning material to the files

    2.____

3. A transfer file is used primarily to

    A. carry records from one office to another
    B. store inactive records
    C. hold records that are constantly used by more than one bureau of an organization
    D. hold confidential records

    3.____

4. When a record is borrowed from the files, the file clerk puts a substitution or *out* card in its place. Of the following, the information that is LEAST commonly placed on the *out* card is

    A. who borrowed the record
    B. when the record was borrowed
    C. why the record was borrowed
    D. what record was borrowed

    4.____

5. It is frequently helpful to file material under two subjects. In such a case the material is filed under one subject and a card indicating where the material is filed is placed under the other subject. This card is known generally as a

    A. follow-up or tickler card   B. guide card
    C. transfer card   D. cross-reference card

    5.____

6. Of the following, for which reason are cross-references necessary in filing?

    A. there is a choice of terms under which the correspondence may be filed
    B. the only filing information contained in the correspondence is the name of the writer
    C. records are immediately visible without searching through the files
    D. persons other than file clerks can easily locate material

7. In filing, a clerk must often attach several papers together before placing them in the files. Usually, the MOST desirable of the following methods of attaching these papers is to

    A. pin them together
    B. staple them together
    C. attach them with a paper clip
    D. glue them together

8. A clerk employed in the central file section of a city department has been requested to obtain a certain card which is kept in an alphabetic file containing several thousand cards, The clerk finds that this card is not in its proper place and that there is no *out* card to aid him in tracing its location. Of the following, the course of action which would be LEAST helpful to him in locating the missing card would be for him to

    A. secure the assistance of his superior
    B. look at several cards filed immediately before and after the place where the missing card should be filed
    C. ask the other clerks in the file section whether they have this card
    D. prepare an *out* card and place it where the missing card should be filed

9. A clerk assigned to file correspondence in a subject file would be MOST concerned with the

    A. name of the sender
    B. main topic of the correspondence
    C. city and state of the sender
    D. date of the correspondence

10. Filing, in a way, is a form of recording. The one of the following which BEST explains this statement is that

    A. no other records are required if a proper filing system is used
    B. important records should, as a rule, be kept in filing cabinets
    C. a good system of record keeping eliminates the necessity for a filing system
    D. filing a letter or document is, in effect, equivalent to making a record of its contents

11. Of the following, a centralized filing system is LEAST suitable for filing

    A. material which is confidential in nature
    B. routine correspondence
    C. periodic reports of the divisions of the department
    D. material used by several divisions of the department

12. *A misplaced record is a lost record.* Of the following, the most valid implication of this statement in regard to office work is that

   A. all records in an office should be filed in strict alphabetical order
   B. accuracy in filing is essential
   C. only one method of filing should be used throughout the office
   D. files should be locked when not in use

12._____

13. Suppose that you are in charge of a unit which maintains a rather intricate filing system. A new file clerk has been added to your staff. Of the following assignments that may be given to this clerk, the one which requires the LEAST amount of knowledge of the filing system is

   A. placing material in the files
   B. removing papers from the files
   C. classifying and coding material for filing
   D. keeping a record of material taken from, and returned to, the files

13._____

14. Which one of the following is the MOST important objective of filing?

   A. Giving a secretary something to do in her spare time
   B. Making it possible to locate information quickly
   C. Providing a place to store unneeded documents
   D. Keeping extra papers from accumulating on workers' desks

14._____

15. Which one of the following BEST describes the usual arrangement of a tickler file?

   A. Alphabetical   B. Chronological
   C. Numerical   D. Geographical

15._____

16. Which one of the following is the LEAST desirable filing practice?

   A. Using staples to keep papers together
   B. Filing all material without regard to date
   C. Keeping a record of all materials removed from the files
   D. Writing filing instructions on each paper prior to filing

16._____

17. The *one* of the following records which it would be MOST advisable to keep in *alphabetical order* is a

   A. continuous listing of phone messages, including time and caller, for your supervisor
   B. listing of individuals currently employed by your agency in a particular title
   C. record of purchases paid for by the petty cash fund
   D. dated record of employees who have borrowed material from the files in your office

17._____

18. Assume that, in an office of a city agency, correspondence is filed, according to the date received, in 12 folders, one for each month of the year. On January 1 of each year, correspondence dated through December 31 of the preceding year is transferred from the active to the inactive files. New folders are then inserted in the active files to contain the correspondence to be filed in the next year. The one of the following which is the chief disadvantage of this method of transferring correspondence from active to inactive files is that

18._____

A. the inactive files may lack the capacity to contain all the correspondence transferred to them
B. the folders prepared each year must be labeled the same as the folders in preceding years
C. some of the correspondence from the preceding year may not be in the active files on January 1
D. some of the correspondence transferred to the inactive files may be referred to as frequently as some of the correspondence in the active files

19. The central filing unit of a certain city department keeps in its files records used by the various bureaus in connection with their daily work. It is desirable for the clerks in this filing unit to refile records as soon as possible after they have been returned by the different bureaus *CHIEFLY* because 19.___

   A. records which are needed can be located most easily if they have been filed
   B. such procedure develops commendable work habits among the employees
   C. records which are not filed immediately are ususally filed incorrectly
   D. the accumulation of records to be filed gives the office a disorderly appearance

20. The active and inactive file material of an office is to be filed in several four-drawer filing cabinets. Of the following, the BEST method of filing the material is, in general, to 20.___

   A. keep inactive material in the upper drawers of the file cabinet so that such material may be easily removed for disposal
   B. keep active material in the upper drawers so that the amount of stooping by clerks using the files is reduced to a minimum
   C. assign drawers in the file cabinets alternately to active and to inactive material so that file material can be transferred easily from the active to the inactive files
   D. assign file cabinets alternately to active and to inactive material so that cross-references between the two types of material can be easily made

---

KEY (CORRECT ANSWERS)

1.	B	11.	A
2.	A	12.	B
3.	B	13.	D
4.	C	14.	B
5.	D	15.	B
6.	A	16.	B
7.	B	17.	B
8.	D	18.	D
9.	B	19.	A
10.	D	20.	B

TEST 2

DIRECTIONS: Each question or incomplete statement is followed by several suggested answers or completions. Select the one that BEST answers the question or completes the statement. *PRINT THE LETTER OF THE CORRECT ANSWER IN THE SPACE AT THE RIGHT.*

1. Suppose you are checking an alphabetical card reference file to locate information about a *George Dyerly*. After checking all the *D's* you can find a card only for a *George Dyrely*. Of the following, the BEST action for you to take is to

    A. check the balance of the file to see if the card you are interested in has been misfiled
    B. check the data on the card to see if it relates to the same person in whom you are interested
    C. correct the spelling of the name on your records and reports to conform to the spelling on the card
    D. reject this reference file as a source of information regarding this person

    1.____

2. Assume that you have been assigned by your supervisor to file some record cards in a cabinet. All the cards in this cabinet are supposed to be kept in strict alphabetical order. You know that important work is being held up because certain cards in this cabinet cannot be located. While filing the records given you, you come across a card which is not in its correct alphabetical place. Of the following, the BEST reason for you to bring this record to the attention of your supervisor is that

    A. errors in filing are more serious than other types of errors
    B. your alertness in locating the card should be rewarded
    C. the filing system may be at fault, rather than the employee who misfiled the card
    D. time may be saved by such action

    2.____

3. A *tickler file* is used CHIEFLY for

    A. unsorted papers which the file clerk has not had time to file
    B. personnel records
    C. pending matters which should receive attention at some particular time
    D. index to cross-referenced material

    3.____

4. A new file clerk who has not become thoroughly familiar with the files is unable to locate *McLeod* in the correspondence files under *Mc* and asks your help. Of the following, the BEST reply to give her is that

    A. there probably is no correspondence in the files for that person
    B. she probably has the name spelled wrong and should verify the spelling
    C. she will probably find the correspondence under *McLeod* as the files are arranged with the prefix *Mc* considered as *Mac* (as if the name were spelled *MacLeod*).
    D. the correspondence folder for *McLeod* has evidently been misplaced or borrowed from the files

    4.____

5. Assume you are in an office which uses a subject filing system. You find that frequently a letter to be filed involves two or three subjects. In filing such a letter, it is MOST important to

    A. file it under the subject that is mentioned first in the letter
    B. prepare cross-references for the subjects covered in the letter

    5.____

C. list all subjects involved on the label of the file folder
D. code the letter to show the main subject and its subdivisions

6. The MOST frequently used filing system in ordinary office practice is the

   A. alphabetic system
   B. numeric system
   C. geographic system
   D. subject system

7. If you wanted to check on the accuracy of the filing in your unit, you would

   A. check all the files thoroughly at regular intervals
   B. watch the clerks while they are filing
   C. glance through filed papers at random
   D. inspect thoroughly a small section of the files selected at random

8. The decision of a secretary to set up and maintain a subject filing system is MOST justified if

   A. speed in placing material in the files is of primary importance
   B. she is generally asked to obtain all the filed material dealing with a particular transaction or topic
   C. the system must be simple enough to permit its use by practically any employee with a little knowledge of filing
   D. there is to be no need to classify material before filing it

9. Several filing operaitons are performed by a secretary in operating and maintaining a subject filing system. Of the filing operations, the two which the secretary can MOST practicably perform at the same time are

   A. coding and placing material in the files
   B. classifying and placing material in the files
   C. placing material in the files and charging out borrowed material
   D. classifying and coding material for the files

10. Of the following systems of filing, the one that is considered the best for safeguarding confidential records is the

    A. alphabetical
    B. numerical
    C. geographical
    D. subject

11. While working in a clinic, you discover some obvious inconsistencies in the filing system as a whole. You also have in mind a corrective measure which you would like to see put into practice. The one of the following which is the MOST acceptable procedure for you to follow is to

    A. try out your new system for a few days to determine its success before discussing it with your supervisor
    B. explain the probable advantages of your proposed plan to your supervisor and secure his approval before making any changes
    C. continue working under the old procedure until the inconsistencies become apparent to the rest of the staff
    D. collect sufficient evidence to prove the obvious inconsistencies in the present filing system in order to convince your supervisor that the system is unsatisfactory

12. Assume that you are in charge of the patients' files in the health center to which you are assigned. The record cards of the individual patients are filed alphabetically according to the name of the patient. You want to make it easier to pick out the cards of those patients who are under treatment for any one of five indicated diseases. Of the following, the procedure which would be MOST helpful for this purpose would be to

    A. insert the card of each patient having one of the five diseases into a special folder
    B. use a different size card for each of the five diseases
    C. use a different color card for each of the five diseases
    D. underline the name of the disease on each card in the file

13. When papers are filed according to the date of their receipt, they are said to be filed

    A. numerically
    B. geographically
    C. chronologically
    D. alphabetically

14. The one of the following which is the MOST important requirement of a good filing system is that

    A. the expense of installation and operation be low
    B. papers be found easily when needed
    C. the system be capable of any amount of expansion which may be necessary in the future
    D. the filing system have a cross-reference index

15. The MAIN purpose of transferring materials from active to inactive files is to

    A. keep current reference files from growing to a size where they become inefficient and unmanageable
    B. distinguish between important business and less important matters
    C. provide a means of storing letters that need not be answered
    D. make sure that there is some way of retrieving information from previous years

16. The one of the following for which a cross-index is *most likely* to be needed is a

    A. file of reference material arranged by subject
    B. file of individual personnel records arranged alphabetically
    C. card file containing addresses and phone numbers for various organizations
    D. supervisor's *tickler file*

17. The CHIEF advantage of a rotary file is that

    A. it holds much more material than a standard file cabinet
    B. it provides a temporary location for material that is due to be placed in the permanent files
    C. items can be easily located and scanned without being removed from the file
    D. less time is required for placing an item on a rotary file than for placing it in a standard upright file

18. In a miscellaneous correspondence folder in a file drawer, it is *usually* MOST helpful if letters are arranged according to

    A. date with the most recent date on the bottom
    B. date with the most recent date on the top

C. subject with the subjects alphabetically arranged
D. name with the names arranged geographically

19. Assume that you are responsible for maintaining the patients' medical record file in the clinic to which you are assigned. Frequently, the other clinics in the health center where you work borrow record cards from your clinic files.
The BEST way for you to avoid difficulty in locating cards which may have been borrowed by other clinics is to

   A. make out a duplicate card for any clinic that wishes to borrow a card from your file
   B. refuse to lend your card to any other clinic unless the other clinic's personnel officer promises to return the card in person
   C. report it to your supervisor if anyone fails to return a card after a reasonable time
   D. have the person who borrows a card fill out an out-of-file card and place it in the file whenever a record card is removed

19.___

20. Suppose that you are given an unalphabetized list of 500 clinic patients and a set of unalphabetized record cards. Your supervisor asks you to determine if there is a record card for each patient whose name is on the list. For you to first arrange the medical record cards in alphabetical order BEFORE checking them with the names on the list is

   A. *desirable;* this will make it easier to check each name on the list against the patients' record cards
   B. *undesirable;* it is just as easy to alphabetize the names on the list as it is to rearrange the record cards
   C. *desirable;* this extra work with the record cards will give you more information about the patients
   D. *undesirable;* adding an extra step to the procedure makes the work too complicated

20.___

KEY (CORRECT ANSWERS)

1.	B	11.	B
2.	D	12.	C
3.	C	13.	C
4.	C	14.	B
5.	B	15.	A
6.	A	16.	A
7.	D	17.	C
8.	B	18.	B
9.	D	19.	D
10.	B	20.	A

TEST 3

DIRECTIONS: Each question or incomplete statement is followed by several suggested answers or completions. Select the one that BEST answers the question or completes the statement. *PRINT THE LETTER OF THE CORRECT ANSWER IN THE SPACE AT THE RIGHT.*

1. Of the following, for which reason are cross-references necessary in filing?   1.____
   A. There is a choice of terms under which the correspondence may be filed.
   B. The only filing information contained in the correspondence is the name of the writer.
   C. Records are immediately visible without searching through the files.
   D. Persons other than file clerks can easily locate material.

2. Suppose that the name files in your office contain filing guides on which appear the letters of the alphabet. The letters X, Y, and Z, unlike the other letters of the alphabet, are grouped together and appear on a single guide. Of the following, the BEST reason for combining these three letters into a single filing unit is probably that   2.____
   A. provision must be made for expanding the file if that should become necessary
   B. there is usually insufficient room for filing guides towards the end of a long file
   C. the letters X, Y, and Z are at the end of the alphabet
   D. relatively few names begin with these letters of the alphabet

3. You are requested by your supervisor to replace each card you take out of the files with an *out-of-file* slip. The *out-of-file* slip indicates which card has been removed from the file and where the card may be found. Of the following the CHIEF value of the *out-of-file* slip is that a clerk looking for a card which happens to have been removed by another clerk   3.____
   A. will know that the card has been returned to the file
   B. can substitute the *out-of-file* slip for the original card
   C. will not waste time searching for the card under the impression that it has been misfiled
   D. is not likely to misfile a card he has been using for some other purpose

4. Suppose that is is the practice, in your department, to file all the correspondence with one individual in a single folder and to file the most recent letters first in the folder. Of the following, the BEST justification for placing the most recent letter first rather than last in the folder is that, in general,   4.____
   A. letters placed in front of a folder are usually less accessible
   B. requests for previous correspondence from the files usually concern letters filed relatively recently
   C. letters in a folder can usually be lcoated most quickly when they are filed in a definite order
   D. filing can usually be accomplished very quickly when letters are placed in a folder without reference to date

5. While filing cards in an alphabetical file, you notice a card which is not in its correct alphabetical order. Of the following the BEST action for you take is to   5.____
   A. show the card to your supervisor and ask him whether that card has been reported lost

B. leave the card where it is, but inform the other clerks who use the file exactly where they may find the card if they need it
C. file a cross-reference card in the place where the card should have been filed
D. make a written notation of where you can find the card in the event that your supervisor asks you for it

6. A new alphabetical name card file covering fifteen file drawers has been set up in your office. Your supervisor asks you to place identifying labels outside each file drawer. Of the following, the BEST rule for you to follow in determining the appropriate label for each drawer is that

    A. the alphabet should be divided equally among the file drawers available
    B. each label should give the beginning and ending points of the cards in that drawer
    C. each drawer should begin with a new letter of the alphabet
    D. no drawer should contain more than two letters of the alphabet

7. One of the administrators in your department cannot find an important letter left on his desk. He believes that the letter may accidentally have been placed among a group of letters sent to you for filing. You look in the file and find the letter filed in its correct place. Of the following, the BEST suggestion for you to make to your supervisor in order to avoid repetition of such incidents is that

    A. file clerks should be permitted to read material they are requested to.
    B. correspondence files should be cross-indexed
    C. a periodic check should be made of the files to locate material inaccurately filed
    D. material which is sent to the file clerk should be marked *OK for filing.*

8. One of your duties is to keep a file of administrative orders by date. Your supervisor often asks you to find the order concerning a particular subject. Since you are rarely able to remember the date of the order, it is necessary for you to search through the entire file. Of the following, the BEST suggestion for you to make to your supervisor for remedying this situation is that

    A. each order bear conspicuously in its upper left hand corner the precise date on which it is issued
    B. old orders be taken from the file and destroyed as soon as they are superseded by new orders, so that the file will not be overcrowded
    C. an alphabetic subject index of orders be prepared so that orders can be located easily by content as well as date
    D. dates be eliminated entirely from orders

9. It is important that every office have a retention and disposal program for filing material. Suppose that you have been appointed administrative assistant in an office with a poorly organized records retention program. In establishing a revised program for the transfer or disposal of records, the step which would logically be taken THIRD in the process is

    A. preparing a safe and inexpensive storage area and setting up an indexing system for records already in storage
    B. determining what papers to retain and for how long a period
    C. taking an inventory of what is filed, where it is filed, how much is filed and how often it is used
    D. moving records from active to inactive files and destroying useless records

10. In evaluating the effectiveness of a filing system, the one of the following criteria which you should consider MOST important is the

    A. safety of material in the event of a fire
    B. ease with which material may be located
    C. quantity of papers which can be filed
    D. extent to which material in the filing system is being used

    10._____

11. In a certain file room it is customary, when removing a record from the files, to insert an out card in its place. A clerk suggests keeping, in addition, a chronological list of all records removed and the names of the employees who have removed them. This suggestion would be of GREATEST value

    A. in avoiding duplication of work
    B. in enabling an employee to refile records
    C. where records are frequently misfiled
    D. where records are frequently kept out longer than necessary

    11._____

12. You are given a large batch of correspondence and asked to obtain the folder on file for each of the senders of these letters. The folders in your file room are kept in numerical order and an alphabetic cross-index file is maintained. Of the following, the BEST procedure would be for you to

    A. look up the numbers in the alphabetic file, then alphabetize the correspondence according to the senders' names and obtain the folders from the numerical file
    B. alphabetize the correspondence according to the senders' names, get the file numbers from the alphabetic file and obtain the folders from the numerical file
    C. alphabetize the correspondence and then look through the numerical file for the proper folders in the order in which your correspondence is arranged
    D. look through the numerical file, pulling out the folders as you come across them

    12._____

13. In filing terminology, coding means

    A. making a preliminary arrangement of names according to caption before bringing them together in final order of arrangement
    B. reading correspondence and determining the proper caption under which it is to be filed
    C. marking a card or paper with symbols or other means of identification to indicate where it is to be placed in the files according to a predetermined plan
    D. placing a card or paper in the files showing where correspondence may be located under another name or title

    13._____

14. A duplex-number system of filing is a(n)

    A. decimal system
    B. arrangement of guides and folders with a definite color scheme to aid in filing and locating material
    C. system of filing by which classified subjects are divided and subdivided by number for the purpose of expansion
    D. method of filing names according to sound instead of spelling

    14._____

15. A set of cards numbered from 1 to 300 has been filed in numerical order in such a way that the highest number is at the front of the file and lowest number is at the rear. It is desired that the cards be reversed to run in ascending order. The BEST of the following methods that can be used in performing this task is to

    A. begin at the front of the file and remove the cards one at a time, placing each one face up on top of the one removed before
    B. begin at the front of the file and remove the cards one at a time, placing each one face down on top of the one removed before
    C. begin at the back of the file and remove the cards in small groups, placing each group face down on top of the group removed before
    D. begin at the back of the file and remove the cards one at a time, placing each one face up on top of the one removed before

16. Confusion regarding the exact location of certain papers missing from files can probably BEST be avoided by

    A. using colored tabs
    B. using the Dewey Decimal System
    C. making files available to few persons
    D. consistently using *out* guides

17. The FIRST step in filing cards alphabetically is to

    A. count the cards
    B. divide the cards into groups of ten
    C. inspect each card to insure that it is filled out completely
    D. rearrange the cards in alphabetical order

18. If you cannot find the folder on Michael Hillston in an alphabetic file, you should

    A. assume that the folder is lost
    B. check other places where the folder could easily have been misfiled, like Hilston and Hillson
    C. look through all of the alphabetic files to see whether the folder was misplaced
    D. return to your other work and check for the folder again the next day

19. Of the following, the type of filing system used in the MOST efficiently run office depends *MOSTLY* on the

    A. way records are used or requested
    B. geographical location of the office
    C. skill of clerical personnel who do the filing
    D. number of filing clerks employed

20. The MOST important reason for well-organized files is to insure that

    A. business papers and records can easily be found
    B. company documents will be arranged alphabetically
    C. file space will be efficiently utilized for business purposes
    D. it is possible to identify the individual who committed any errors

KEY (CORRECT ANSWERS)

1. A
2. D
3. C
4. B
5. A

6. B
7. D
8. C
9. A
10. B

11. D
12. B
13. C
14. C
15. A

16. D
17. D
18. B
19. A
20. A

RECORD KEEPING
EXAMINATION SECTION
TEST 1

DIRECTIONS: Each question or incomplete statement is followed by several suggested answers or completions. Select the one that BEST answers the question or completes the statement. *PRINT THE LETTER OF THE CORRECT ANSWER IN THE SPACE AT THE RIGHT.*

Questions 1-15.

DIRECTIONS: Questions 1 through 15 are to be answered on the basis of the following list of company names below. Arrange a file alphabetically, word-by-word, disregarding punctuation, conjunctions, and apostrophes. Then answer the questions.
A Bee C Reading Materials
ABCO Parts
A Better Course for Test Preparation
AAA Auto Parts Co.
A-Z Auto Parts, Inc.
Aabar Books
Abbey, Joanne
Boman-Sylvan Law Firm
BMW Autowerks
C Q Service Company
Chappell-Murray, Inc.
E&E Life Insurance
Emcrisco
Gigi Arts
Gordon, Jon & Associates
SOS Plumbing
Schmidt, J.B. Co.

1. Which of these files should appear FIRST?   1.____

   A. ABCO Parts
   B. A Bee C Reading Materials
   C. A Better Course for Test Preparation
   D. AAA Auto Parts Co.

2. Which of these files should appear SECOND?   2.____

   A. A-Z Auto Parts, Inc.
   B. A Bee C Reading Materials
   C. A Better Course for Test Preparation
   D. AAA Auto Parts Co.

3. Which of these files should appear THIRD?   3.____

   A. ABCO Parts
   B. A Bee C Reading Materials
   C. Aabar Books
   D. AAA Auto Parts Co.

4. Which of these files should appear FOURTH?   4.___

   A. Aabar Books
   B. ABCO Parts
   C. Abbey, Joanne
   D. AAA Auto Parts Co.

5. Which of these files should appear LAST?   5.___

   A. Gordon, Jon & Associates
   B. Gigi Arts
   C. Schmidt, J.B. Co.
   D. SOS Plumbing

6. Which of these files should appear between A-Z Auto Parts, Inc. and Abbey, Joanne?   6.___

   A. A Bee C Reading Materials
   B. AAA Auto Parts Co.
   C. ABCO Parts
   D. A Better Course for Test Preparation

7. Which of these files should appear between ABCO Parts and Aabar Books?   7.___

   A. A Bee C Reading Materials
   B. Abbey, Joanne
   C. Aabar Books
   D. A-Z Auto Parts

8. Which of these files should appear between Abbey, Joanne and Boman-Sylvan Law Firm?   8.___

   A. A Better Course for Test Preparation
   B. BMW Autowerks
   C. Chappell-Murray, Inc.
   D. Aabar Books

9. Which of these files should appear between Abbey, Joanne and C Q Service?   9.___

   A. A-Z Auto Parts,Inc.   B. BMW Autowerks
   C. Choices A and B   D. Chappell-Murray, Inc.

10. Which of these files should appear between C Q Service Company and Emcrisco?   10.___

    A. Chappell-Murray, Inc.   B. E&E Life Insurance
    C. Gigi Arts   D. Choices A and B

11. Which of these files should NOT appear between C Q Service Company and E&E Life Insurance?   11.___

    A. Gordon, Jon & Associates
    B. Emcrisco
    C. Gigi Arts
    D. All of the above

12. Which of these files should appear between Chappell-Murray Inc., and Gigi Arts? 12.____

    A. CQ Service Inc. E&E Life Insurance, and Emcrisco
    B. Emcrisco, E&E Life Insurance, and Gordon, Jon & Associates
    C. E&E Life Insurance and Emcrisco
    D. Emcrisco and Gordon, Jon & Associates

13. Which of these files should appear between Gordon, Jon & Associates and SOS Plumbing? 13.____

    A. Gigi Arts   B. Schmidt, J.B. Co.
    C. Choices A and B   D. None of the above

14. Each of the choices lists the four files in their proper alphabetical order except 14.____

    A. E&E Life Insurance; Gigi Arts; Gordon, Jon & Associates; SOS Plumbing
    B. E&E Life Insurance; Emcrisco; Gigi Arts; SOS Plumbing
    C. Emcrisco; Gordon, Jon & Associates; SOS Plumbing; Schmidt, J.B. Co.
    D. Emcrisco; Gigi Arts; Gordon, Jon & Associates; SOS Plumbing

15. Which of the choices lists the four files in their proper alphabetical order? 15.____

    A. Gigi Arts; Gordon, Jon & Associates; SOS Plumbing; Schmidt, J.B. Co.
    B. Gordon, Jon & Associates; Gigi Arts; Schmidt, J.B. Co.; SOS Plumbing
    C. Gordon, Jon & Associates; Gigi Arts; SOS Plumbing; Schmidt, J.B. Co.
    D. Gigi Arts; Gordon, Jon & Associates; Schmidt, J.B. Co.; SOS Plumbing

16. The alphabetical filing order of two businesses with identical names is determined by the 16.____

    A. length of time each business has been operating
    B. addresses of the businesses
    C. last name of the company president
    D. none of the above

17. In an alphabetical filing system, if a business name includes a number, it should be 17.____

    A. disregarded
    B. considered a number and placed at the end of an alphabetical section
    C. treated as though it were written in words and alphabetized accordingly
    D. considered a number and placed at the beginning of an alphabetical section

18. If a business name includes a contraction (such as *don't* or *it's*), how should that word be treated in an alphabetical filing system? 18.____

    A. Divide the word into its separate parts and treat it as two words.
    B. Ignore the letters that come after the apostrophe.
    C. Ignore the word that contains the contraction.
    D. Ignore the apostrophe and consider all letters in the contraction.

19. In what order should the parts of an address be considered when using an alphabetical filing system? 19.____

    A. City or town; state; street name; house or building number
    B. State; city or town; street name; house or building number
    C. House or building number; street name; city or town; state
    D. Street name; city or town; state

20. A business record should be cross-referenced when a(n)

   A. organization is known by an abbreviated name
   B. business has a name change because of a sale, incorporation, or other reason
   C. business is known by a *coined* or common name which differs from a dictionary spelling
   D. all of the above

21. A geographical filing system is MOST effective when

   A. location is more important than name
   B. many names or titles sound alike
   C. dealing with companies who have offices all over the world
   D. filing personal and business files

Questions 22-25.

DIRECTIONS: Questions 22 through 25 are to be answered on the basis of the list of items below, which are to be filed geographically. Organize the items geographically and then answer the questions.

   1. University Press at Berkeley, U.S.
   2. Maria Sanchez, Mexico City, Mexico
   3. Great Expectations Ltd. in London, England
   4. Justice League, Cape Town, South Africa, Africa
   5. Crown Pearls Ltd. in London, England
   6. Joseph Prasad in London, England

22. Which of the following arrangements of the items is composed according to the policy of: *Continent, Country, City, Firm or Individual Name?*

   A. 5, 3, 4, 6, 2, 1   B. 4, 5, 3, 6, 2, 1
   C. 1, 4, 5, 3, 6, 2   D. 4, 5, 3, 6, 1, 2

23. Which of the following files is arranged according to the policy of: *Continent, Country, City, Firm or Individual Name?*

   A. South Africa. Africa. Cape Town. Justice League
   B. Mexico. Mexico City, Maria Sanchez
   C. North America. United States. Berkeley. University Press
   D. England. Europe. London. Prasad, Joseph

24. Which of the following arrangements of the items is composed according to the policy of: *Country, City, Firm or Individual Name?*

   A. 5, 6, 3, 2, 4, 1   B. 1, 5, 6, 3, 2, 4
   C. 6, 5, 3, 2, 4, 1   D. 5, 3, 6, 2, 4, 1

25. Which of the following files is arranged according to a policy of: *Country, City, Firm or Individual Name?*

   A. England. London. Crown Pearls Ltd.
   B. North America. United States. Berkeley. University Press
   C. Africa. Cape Town. Justice League
   D. Mexico City. Mexico. Maria Sanchez

26. Under which of the following circumstances would a phonetic filing system be MOST effective? 26.____

    A. When the person in charge of filing can't spell very well
    B. With large files with names that sound alike
    C. With large files with names that are spelled alike
    D. All of the above

Questions 27-29.

DIRECTIONS: Questions 27 through 29 are to be answered on the basis of the following list of numerical files.
   1. 391-023-100
   2. 361-132-170
   3. 385-732-200
   4. 381-432-150
   5. 391-632-387
   6. 361-423-303
   7. 391-123-271

27. Which of the following arrangements of the files follows a consecutive-digit system? 27.____

    A. 2, 3, 4, 1   B. 1, 5, 7, 3
    C. 2, 4, 3, 1   D. 3, 1, 5, 7

28. Which of the following arrangements follows a terminal-digit system? 28.____

    A. 1, 7, 2, 4, 3   B. 2, 1, 4, 5, 7
    C. 7, 6, 5, 4, 3   D. 1, 4, 2, 3, 7

29. Which of the following lists follows a middle-digit system? 29.____

    A. 1, 7, 2, 6, 4, 5, 3   B. 1, 2, 7, 4, 6, 5, 3
    C. 7, 2, 1, 3, 5, 6, 4   D. 7, 1, 2, 4, 6, 5, 3

Questions 30-31.

DIRECTIONS: Questions 30 and 31 are to be answered on the basis of the following information.
   1. Reconfirm Laura Bates appointment with James Caldecort on December 12 at 9:30 A.M.
   2. Laurence Kinder contact Julia Lucas on August 3 and set up a meeting for week of September 23 at 4 P.M.
   3. John Lutz contact Larry Waverly on August 3 and set up appointment for September 23 at 9:30 A.M.
   4. Call for tickets for Gerry Stanton August 21 for New Jersey on September 23, flight 143 at 4:43 P.M.

30. A chronological file for the above information would be 30.____

    A. 4, 3, 2, 1 B. 3, 2, 4, 1
    C. 4, 2, 3, 1 D. 3, 1, 2, 4

31. Using the above information, a chronological file for the date of September 23 would be 31.____

    A. 2, 3, 4   B. 3, 1, 4   C. 3, 2, 4   D. 4, 3, 2

Questions 32-34.

DIRECTIONS: Questions 32 through 34 are to be answered on the basis of the following information.
1. Call Roger Epstein, Ashoke Naipaul, Jon Anderson, and Sarah Washington on April 19 at 1:00 P.M. to set up meeting with Alika D'Ornay for June 6 in New York.
2. Call Martin Ames before noon on April 19 to confirm afternoon meeting with Bob Greenwood on April 20th
3. Set up meeting room at noon for 2:30 P.M. meeting on April 19th;
4. Ashley Stanton contact Bob Greenwood at 9:00 A.M. on April 20 and set up meeting for June 6 at 8:30 A.M.
5. Carol Guiland contact Shelby Van Ness during afternoon of April 20 and set up meeting for June 6 at 10:00 A.M.
6. Call airline and reserve tickets on June 6 for Roger Epstein trip *to* Denver on July 8
7. Meeting at 2:30 P.M. on April 19th

32. A chronological file for all of the above information would be 32.____

    A. 2, 1, 3, 7, 5, 4, 6   B. 3, 7, 2, 1, 4, 5, 6
    C. 3, 7, 1, 2, 5, 4, 6   D. 2, 3, 1, 7, 4, 5, 6

33. A chronological file for the date of April 19th would be 33.____

    A. 2, 3, 7, 1   B. 2, 3, 1, 7
    C. 7, 1, 3, 2   D. 3, 7, 1, 2

34. Add the following information to the file, and then create a chronological file for April 20th: 34.____
    8. April 20: 3:00 P.M. meeting between Bob Greenwood and Martin Ames.

    A. 4, 5, 8   B. 4, 8, 5   C. 8, 5, 4   D. 5, 4, 8

35. The PRIMARY advantage of computer records filing over a manual system is 35.____

    A. speed of retrieval   B. accuracy
    C. cost   D. potential file loss

KEY (CORRECT ANSWERS)

1.	B	16.	B
2.	C	17.	C
3.	D	18.	D
4.	A	19.	A
5.	D	20.	D
6.	C	21.	A
7.	B	22.	B
8.	B	23.	C
9.	C	24.	D
10.	D	25.	A
11.	D	26.	B
12.	C	27.	C
13.	B	28.	D
14.	C	29.	A
15.	D	30.	B

31. C
32. D
33. B
34. A
35. A

NAME AND NUMBER CHECKING

EXAMINATION SECTION
TEST 1

DIRECTIONS: This test is designed to measure your speed and accuracy. You are urged to work both quickly and accurately and to do correctly as many lists as you can in the time allowed. The test consists of lists of pairs of names and numbers. Count the number of IDENTICAL pairs in each list. Then, select the correct number, 1, 2, 3, 4, or 5, and indicate your choice by circling the corresponding number on your answer paper, Two sample questions are presented for your guidance, together with the correct solutions.

SAMPLE QUESTIONS

SAMPLE LIST A

		CIRCLE CORRECT ANSWER
Adelphi College	- Adelphia College	1 2 3 4 5
Braxton Corp.	- Braxeton Corp.	
Wassaic State School	- Wassaic State School	
Central Islip State Hospital	- Central Isllip State	
Greenwich House	- Greenwich House	

NOTE that there are only two correct pairs - Wassaic State School and Greenwich House. Therefore, the CORRECT answer is 2.

SAMPLE LIST B

78453694	- 78453684	1 2 3 4 5
784530	- 784530	
533	- 534	
67845	- 67845	
2368745	- 2368755	

NOTE that there are only two correct pairs - 784530 and 67845. Therefore, the CORRECT answer is 2.

LIST 1

98654327	- 98654327	1 2 3 4 5
74932564	- 74922564	
61438652	- 61438652	
01297653	- 01287653	
1865439765	- 1865439765	

LIST 2

478362	- 478363	1 2 3 4 5
278354792	- 278354772	
9327	- 9327	
297384625	- 27384625	
6428156	- 6428158	

LIST 3   CIRCLE
                                                 CORRECT ANSWER
    Abbey House   - Abbey House   1 2 3 4 5
    Actors' Fund Home   - Actor's Fund Home
    Adrian Memorial   - Adrian Memorial
    A. Clayton Powell Home   - Clayton Powell House
    Abott E. Kittredge Club - Abbott E. Kitteredge Club

LIST 4
    3682   - 3692   1 2 3 4 5
    21937453829   - 31937453829
    723   - 733
    2763920   - 2763920
    47293   - 47293

LIST 5
    Adra House   - Adra House   1 2 3 4 5
    Adolescents' Court   - Adolescents' Court
    Cliff Villa   - Cliff Villa
    Clark Neighborhood House - Clark Neighborhood House
    Alma Mathews House   - Alma Mathews House

LIST 6
    28734291   - 28734271   1 2 3 4 5
    63810263849   - 63810263846
    26831027   - 26831027
    368291   - 368291
    7238102637   - 7238102637

LIST 7
    Albion State T.S.   - Albion State T.C.   1 2 3 4 5
    Clara de Hirsch Home   - Clara De Hirsch Home
    Alice Carrington Royce   - Alice Carington Royce
    Alice Chopin Nursery   - Alice Chapin Nursery
    Lighthouse Eye Clinic   - Lighthouse Eye Clinic

LIST 8
    327   - 329   1 2 3 4 5
    712438291026   - 712438291026
    2753829142   - 275382942
    826287   - 826289
    26435162839   - 26435162839

LIST 9
    Letchworth Village   - Letchworth Village   1 2 3 4 5
    A.A.A.E. Inc.   - A.A.A.E. Inc.
    Clear Pool Camp   - Clear Pool Camp
    A.M.M.L.A. Inc.   - A.M.M.L.A. Inc.
    J.G. Harbard   - J.G. Harbord

| | | CIRCLE |
| | | CORRECT ANSWER |

LIST 10
    8254   - 8256   1   2   3   4   5
    2641526   - 2641526
    4126389012   - 4126389102
    725   - 725
    76253917287   - 76253917287

LIST 11
    Attica State Prison   - Attica State Prison   1   2   3   4   5
    Nellie Murrah   - Nellie Murrah
    Club Marshall   - Club Marshal
    Assissium Casea-Maria   - Assissium Casa-Maria
    The Homestead   - The Homestead

LIST 12
    2691   - 2691   1   2   3   4   5
    623819253627   - 623819253629
    28637   - 28937
    278392736   - 278392736
    52739   - 52739

LIST 13
    A.I.C.P. Boys Camp   - A.I.C.P. Boy's Camp   1   2   3   4   5
    Einar Chrystie   - Einar Christyie
    Astoria Center   - Astoria Center
    G. Frederick Brown   - G. Federick Browne
    Vacation Service   - Vacation Services

LIST 14
    728352689   - 728352688   1   2   3   4   5
    643728   - 643728
    37829176   - 37827196
    8425367   - 8425369
    65382018   - 65382018

LIST 15
    E.S. Streim   - E.S. Strim   1   2   3   4   5
    Charles E. Higgins   - Charles E. Higgins
    Baluvelt, N.Y.   - Blauwelt, N.Y.
    Roberta Magdalen   - Roberto Magdalen
    Ballard School   - Ballard School

LIST 16
    7382   - 7392   1   2   3   4   5
    281374538299   - 291374538299
    623   - 633
    6273730   - 6273730
    63392   - 63392

CIRCLE CORRECT ANSWER

LIST 17
    Orrin Otis   - Orrin Otis   1   2   3   4   5
    Barat Settlement   - Barat Settlemen
    Emmanuel House   - Emmanuel House
    William T. McCreery - William T. McCreery
    Seamen's Home   - Seaman's Home

LIST 18
    72824391   - 72834371   1   2   3   4   5
    3729106237   - 37291106237
    82620163849   - 82620163846
    37638921   - 37638921
    82631027   - 82631027

LIST 19
    Commonwealth Fund   - Commonwealth Fund   1   2   3   4   5
    Anne Johnsen   - Anne Johnson
    Bide-a-Wee Home   - Bide-a-Wee Home
    Riverdale-on-Hudson   - Riverdal-on-Hudson
    Bialystoker Home   - Bailystoker Home

LIST 20
    9271   - 9271   1   2   3   4   5
    392918352627   - 392018852629
    72637   - 72637
    927392736   - 927392736
    92739   - 92739

LIST 21
    Charles M. Stump   - Charles M. Stump   1   2   3   4   5
    Bourne Workshop   - Buorne Workshop
    B'nai Bi'rith   - B'nai Brith
    Poppenhuesen Institute   - Poppenheusen Institute
    Consular Service   - Consular Service

LIST 22
    927352689   - 927352688   1   2   3   4   5
    647382   - 648382
    93729176   - 93727196
    649536718   - 649536718
    5835367   - 5835369

LIST 23
    L.S. Bestend   - L.S. Bestent   1   2   3   4   5
    Hirsch Mfg. Co.   - Hircsh Mfg. Co.
    F.H. Storrs   - F.P. Storrs
    Camp Wassaic   - Camp Wassaic
    George Ballingham - George Ballingham

LIST 24
 372846392048 - 372846392048
 334   - 334
 7283524678   - 7283524678
 7283   - 7283
 7283629372   - 7283629372

CIRCLE CORRECT ANSWER
1 2 3 4 5

LIST 25
 Dr. Stiles Company - Dr. Stills Company
 Frances Hunsdon - Frances Hunsdon
 Northrop Barrert - Nothrup Barrent
 J. D. Brunjes   - J. D. Brunjes
 Theo. Claudel & Co. - Theo. Claudel co.

1 2 3 4 5

KEY (CORRECT ANSWERS)

1.	3	11.	3
2.	1	12.	3
3.	2	13.	1
4.	2	14.	2
5.	5	15.	2
6.	3	16.	2
7.	1	17.	3
8.	2	18.	2
9.	4	19.	2
10.	3	20.	4

21.	2
22.	1
23.	2
24.	5
25.	2

TEST 2

DIRECTIONS: This test is designed to measure your speed and accuracy. You are urged to work both quickly and accurately and to do correctly as many lists as you can in the time allowed. The test consists of lists of pairs of names and numbers. Count the number of IDENTICAL pairs in each list. Then, select the correct number, 1, 2, 3, 4, or 5, and indicate your choice by circling the corresponding number on your answer paper, Two sample questions are presented for your guidance, together with the correct solutions.

		CIRCLE CORRECT ANSWER
LIST 1		
82728	- 82738	1 2 3 4 5
82736292637	- 82736292639	
728	- 738	
83926192527	- 83726192529	
82736272	- 82736272	
LIST 2		
L. Pietri	- L. Pietri	1 2 3 4 5
Mathewson, L.F.	- Mathewson, L.F.	
Funk & Wagnall	- Funk &. Wagnalls	
Shimizu, Sojio	- Shimizu, Sojio	
Filing Equipment Bureau	- Filing Equipment Buraeu	
LIST 3		
63801829374	- 63801839474	1 2 3 4 5
283577657	- 283577657	
65689	- 65689	
3457892026	- 3547893026	
2779	- 2778	
LIST 4		
August Caille	- August Caille	1 2 3 4 5
The Well-Fare Service	- The Wel-Fare Service	
K.L.M. Process Co.	- R.L.M. Process Co.	
Merrill Littell	- Merrill Littell	
Dodd & Sons	- Dodd & Son	
LIST 5		
998745732	- 998745733	1 2 3 4 5
723	- 723	
463849102983	- 463849102983	
8570	- 8570	
279012	- 279012	
LIST 6		
M. A. Wender	- M.A. Winder	1 2 3 4 5
Minneapolis Supply Co.	- Minneapolis Supply Co.	
Beverly Hills Corp	- Beverley Hills Corp.	
Trafalgar Square	- Trafalgar Square	
Phifer, D.T.	- Phiefer, D.T.	

2 (#2)

		CIRCLE CORRECT ANSWER

LIST 7
    7834629   - 7834629   1 2 3 4 5
    3549806746   - 3549806746
    97802564   - 97892564
    689246   - 688246
    2578024683   - 2578024683

LIST 8
    Scadrons'   - Scadrons'   1 2 3 4 5
    Gensen & Bro.   - Genson & Bro.
    Firestone Co.   - Firestone Co.
    H.L. Eklund   - H.L. Eklund
    Oleomargarine Co. - Oleomargarine Co.

LIST 9
    782039485618   - 782039485618   1 2 3 4 5
    53829172639   - 63829172639
    892   - 892
    82937482   - 829374820
    52937456   - 53937456

LIST 10
    First Nat'l Bank   - First Nat'l Bank   1 2 3 4 5
    Sedgwick Machine Works - Sedgewick Machine Works
    Hectographia Co.   - Hectographia Corp.
    Levet Bros.   - Levet Bros.
    Multistamp Co.,Inc.   - Multistamp Co.,Inc.

LIST 11
    7293   - 7293   1 2 3 4 5
    6382910293   - 6382910292
    981928374012   - 981928374912
    58293   - 58393
    18203649271   - 283019283745

LIST 12
    Lowrey Lb'r Co.   - Lowrey Lb'r Co.   1 2 3 4 5
    Fidelity Service   - Fidelity Service
    Reumann, J.A.   - Reumann, J.A.
    Duophoto Ltd.   - Duophotos Ltd.
    John Jarratt   - John Jaratt

LIST 13
    6820384   - 6820384   1 2 3 4 5
    383019283745   - 383019283745
    63927102   - 63928102
    91029354829   - 91029354829
    58291728   - 58291728

LIST 14
    Standard Press Co.   - Standard Press Co.   CIRCLE CORRECT ANSWER
    Reliant Mf'g. Co.   - Relant Mf'g Co.
    M.C. Lynn   - M.C. Lynn
    J. Fredericks Company   - G. Fredericks Company
    Wandermann, B.S.   - Wanderman, B.S.

1 2 3 4 5

LIST 15
    4283910293   - 4283010203
    992018273648   - 992018273848
    620   - 629
    752937273   - 752937373
    5392   - 5392

1 2 3 4 5

LIST 16
    Waldorf Hotel   - Waldorf Hotel
    Aaron Machinery Co.   - Aaron Machinery Co.
    Caroline Ann Locke   - Caroline Anne Locke
    McCabe Mfg. Co.   - McCabe Mfg. Co.
    R.L. Landres   - R.L. Landers

1 2 3 4 5

LIST 17
    68391028364   - 68391028394
    68293   - 68293
    739201   - 739201
    72839201   - 72839211
    739917   - 739719

1 2 3 4 5

LIST 18
    Balsam M.M.   - Balsamm, M.M.
    Steinway & Co.   - Stienway & M. Co.
    Eugene Elliott   - Eugene A. Elliott
    Leonard Loan Co.   - Leonard Loan Co.
    Frederick Morgan   - Frederick Morgen

1 2 3 4 5

LIST 19
    8929   - 9820
    392836472829   - 392836472829
    462   - 462 2039271
    827   - 2039276837
    53829   - 54829

1 2 3 4 5

LIST 20
    Danielson's Hofbrau   - Danielson's Hafbrau
    Edward A. Truarme   - Edward A. Truame
    Insulite Co.   - Insulite Co.
    Reisler Shoe Corp,   - Rielser Shoe Corp.
    L.L. Thompson   - L.L. Thompson

1 2 3 4 5

LIST 21
   92839102837   - 92839102837
   58891028   - 58891028
   7291728   - 7291928
   272839102839   - 272839102839
   428192   - 428102

CIRCLE CORRECT ANSWER 1 2 3 4 5

LIST 22
   K.L. Veiller   - K.L. Veiller
   Webster, Roy   - Webster, Ray
   Drasner Spring Co.   - Drasner Spring Co.
   Edward J. Cravenport   - Edward J. Cravanport
   Harold Field   - Harold A. Field

1 2 3 4 5

LIST 23
   2293   - 2293
   4283910293   - 5382910292
   871928374012   - 871928374912
   68293   - 68393
   8120364927   - 81293649271

1 2 3 4 5

LIST 24
   Tappe, Inc   - Tappe, Inc.
   A.M. Wentingworth   - A.M. Wentinworth
   Scott A. Elliott   - Scott A. Elliott
   Echeverria Corp.   - Echeverria Corp.
   Bradford Victor Company   - Bradford Victer Company

1 2 3 4 5

LIST 25
   4820384   - 4820384
   393019283745   - 283919283745
   63927102   - 63927102
   91029354829   - 91029354829
   48291728   - 48291728

1 2 3 4 5

KEY (CORRECT ANSWERS)

1.	1	11.	1
2.	3	12.	3
3.	2	13.	4
4.	2	14.	2
5.	4	15.	1
6.	2	16.	3
7.	3	17.	2
8.	4	18.	1
9.	3	19.	2
10.	3	20.	2

21. 3
22. 2
23. 1
24. 3
25. 4

CODING
EXAMINATION SECTION
TEST 1

COMMENTARY

An ingenious question-type called coding, involving elements of alphabetizing, filing, name and number comparison, and evaluative judgment and application, has currently won wide acceptance in testing circles for measuring clerical aptitude and general ability, particularly on the senior (middle) grades (levels).

While the directions for this question-type usually vary in detail, the candidate is generally asked to consider groups of names, codes, and numbers, and, then, according to a given plan, to arrange codes in alphabetic order; to arrange these in numerical sequence; to re-arrange columns of names and numbers in correct order; to espy errors in coding; to choose the correct coding arrangement in consonance with the given directions and examples, etc.

This question-type appears to have few parameters in respect to form, substance, or degree of difficulty.

Accordingly, acquaintance with, and practice in the coding question is recommended for the serious candidate.

DIRECTIONS: Column I consists of serial numbers of dollar bills. Column II shows different ways of arranging the corresponding serial numbers.
The serial numbers of dollar bills in Column I begin and end with a capital letter and have an eight-digit number in between. The serial numbers in Column I are to be arranged according to the following rules:

First: In alphabetical order according to the first letter.

Second: When two or more serial numbers have the same first letter, in alphabetical order according to the last letter.

Third: When two or more serial numbers have the same first *and* last letters, in numerical order, beginning with the lowest number

The serial numbers in Column I are numbered (1) through (5) in the order in which they are listed. In Column II the numbers (1) through (5) are arranged in four different ways to show different arrangements of the corresponding serial numbers. Choose the answer in Column II in which the serial numbers are arranged according to the above rules.

Column I	Column II
1. E75044127B	A. 4, 1, 3, 2, 5
2. B96399104A	B. 4, 1, 2, 3, 5
3. B93939086A	C. 4, 3, 2, 5, 1
4. B47064465H	D. 3, 2, 5, 4, 1

In the sample question, the four serial numbers starting with B should be put before the serial number starting with E. The serial numbers starting with B and ending with A should be put before the serial number starting with B and ending with H. The three serial numbers starting with B and ending with A should be listed in numerical order, beginning with the lowest number. The correct way to arrange the serial numbers therefore is:

3. B93939086A
2. B96399104A
5. B99040922A
4. B47064465H
1. E75044127B

Since the order of arrangement is 3, 2, 5, 4, 1, the answer to the sample question is D.

	Column I		Column II	
1.	1. D89143888P	A.	3, 5, 2, 1, 4	1.___
	2. D98143838B	B.	3, 1, 4, 5, 2	
	3. D89113883B	C.	4, 2, 3, 1, 5	
	4. D89148338P	D.	4, 1, 3, 5, 2	
	5. D89148388B			
2.	1. W62455599E	A.	2, 4, 3, 1, 5	2.___
	2. W62455090F	B.	3, 1, 5, 2, 4	
	3. W62405099E	C.	5, 3, 1, 4, 2	
	4. V62455097F	D.	5, 4, 3, 1, 2	
	5. V62405979E			
3.	1. N74663826M	A.	2, 4, 5, 3, 1	3.___
	2. M74633286M	B.	2, 5, 4, 1, 3	
	3. N76633228N	C.	1, 2, 5, 3, 4	
	4. M76483686N	D.	2, 5, 1, 4, 3	
	5. M74636688M			
4.	1. P97560324B	A.	1, 5, 2, 3, 4	4.___
	2. R97663024B	B.	3, 1, 4, 5, 2	
	3. P97503024E	C.	1, 5, 3, 2, 4	
	4. R97563240E	D.	1, 5; 2* 3, 4	
	5. P97652304B			
5.	1. H92411165G	A.	2, 5, 3, 4, 1	5.___
	2. A92141465G	B.	3, 4, 2, 5, 1	
	3. H92141165C	C.	3, 2, 1, 5, 4	
	4. H92444165C	D.	3, 1, 2, 5, 4	
	5. A92411465G			
6.	1. X90637799S	A.	4, 3, 5, 2, 1	6.___
	2. N90037696S	B.	5, 4, 2, 1, 3	
	3. Y90677369B	C.	5, 2, 4, 1, 3	
	4. X09677693B	D.	5, 2, 3, 4, 1	
	5. M09673699S			
7.	1. K78425174L	A.	4, 2, 1, 3, 5	7.___
	2. K78452714C	B.	2, 3, 5, 4, 1	
	3. K78547214N	C.	1, 4, 2, 3, 5	
	4. K78442774C	D.	4, 2, 1, 5, 3	
	5. K78547724M			
8.	1. P18736652U	A.	1, 3, 4, 5, 2	8.___
	2. P18766352V	B.	1, 5, 2, 3, 4	
	3. T17686532U	C.	3, 4, 5, 1, 2	
	4. T17865523U	D.	5, 2, 1, 3, 4	
	5. P18675332V			
9.	1. L51138101K	A.	1, 5, 3, 2, 4	9.___
	2. S51138001R	B.	1, 3, 5, 2, 4	
	3. S51188111K	C.	1, 5, 2, 4, 3	
	4. S51183110R	D.	2, 5, 1, 4, 3	
	5. L51188100R			

3 (#1)

	Column I	Column II	

10. 1. J28475336D
    2. T28775363D
    3. J27843566P
    4. T27834563P
    5. J28435536D

  A. 5, 1, 2, 3, 4
  B. 4, 3, 5, 1, 2
  C. 1, 5, 2, 4, 3
  D. 5, 1, 3, 2, 4

10.____

11. 1. S55126179E
    2. R55136177Q
    3. P55126177R
    4. S55126178R
    5. R55126180P

  A. 1, 5, 2, 3, 4
  B. 3, 4, 1, 5, 2
  C. 3, 5, 2, 1, 4
  D. 4, 3, 1, 5, 2

11.____

12. 1. T64217813Q
    2. I642178170
    3. T642178180
    4. I64217811Q
    5. T64217816Q

  A. 4, 1, 3, 2, 5
  B. 2, 4, 3, 1, 5
  C. 4, 1, 5, 2, 3
  D. 2, 3, 4, 1, 5

12.____

13. 1. B33886897B
    2. B38386882B
    3. D33389862B
    4. D33336887D
    5. B38888697D

  A. 5, 1, 3, 4, 2
  B. 1, 2, 5, 3, 4
  C. 1, 2, 5, 4, 3
  D. 2, 1, 4, 5, 3

13.____

14. 1. E11664554M
    2. F11164544M
    3. F11614455N
    4. E11665454M
    5. F16161545N

  A. 4, 1, 2, 5, 3
  B. 2, 4, 1, 5, 3
  C. 4, 2, 1, 3, 5
  D. 1, 4, 2, 3, 5

14.____

15. 1. C86611355W
    2. C68631533V
    3. G88633331W
    4. C68833515V
    5. G68833511W

  A. 2, 4, 1, 5, 3
  B. 1, 2, 4, 3, 5
  C. 1, 2, 5, 4, 3
  D. 1, 2, 4, 3, 5

15.____

16. 1. R73665312J
    2. P73685512J
    3. P73968511J
    4. R73665321K
    5. R63985211K

  A. 3, 2, 1, 4, 5
  B. 2, 3, 5, 1, 4
  C. 2, 3, 1, 5, 4
  D. 3, 1, 5, 2, 4

16.____

17. 1. X33661222U
    2. Y83961323V
    3. Y88991123V
    4. X33691233U
    5. X38691333U

  A. 1, 4, 5, 2, 3
  B. 4, 5, 1, 3, 2
  C. 4, 5, 1, 2, 3
  D. 4, 1, 5, 2, 3

17.____

	Column I	Column II	

	Column I		Column II	
18.	1. B22838847W	A.	4, 5, 2, 3, 1	18.___
	2. B28833874V	B.	4, 2, 5, 1, 3	
	3. B22288344X	C.	4, 5, 2, 1, 3	
	4. B28238374V	D.	4, 1, 5, 2, 3	
	5. B28883347V			
19.	1. H44477447G	A.	1, 3, 5, 4, 2	19.___
	2. H47444777G	B.	3, 1, 5, 2, 4	
	3. H74777477C	C.	1, 4, 2, 3, 5	
	4. H44747447G	D.	3, 5, 1, 4, 2	
	5. H77747447C			
20.	1. G11143447G	A.	3, 5, 1, 4, 2	20.___
	2. G15133388C	B.	1, 4, 3, 2, 5	
	3. C15134378G	C.	5, 3, 4, 2, 1	
	4. G11534477C	D.	4, 3, 1, 2, 5	
	5. C15533337C			
21.	1. J96693369F	A.	4, 3, 2, 5, 1	21.___
	2. J66939339F	B.	2, 5, 4, 1, 3	
	3. J96693693E	C.	2, 5, 4, 3, 1	
	4. J96663933E	D.	3, 4, 5, 2, 1	
	5. J69639363F			
22.	1. L15567834Z	A.	3, 1, 5, 2, 4	22.___
	2. P11587638Z	B.	1, 3, 5, 4, 2	
	3. M51567688Z	C.	1, 3, 5, 2, 4	
	4. O55578784Z	D.	3, 1, 5, 4, 2	
	5. N53588783Z			
23.	1. C83261824G	A.	2, 4, 1, 5, 3	23.___
	2. C78361833C	B.	4, 2, 1, 3, 5	
	3. G83261732G	C.	3, 1, 5, 2, 4	
	4. C88261823C	D.	2, 3, 5, 1, 4	
	5. G83261743C			
24.	1. A11710107H	A.	2, 1, 4, 3, 5	24.___
	2. H17110017A	B.	3, 1, 5, 2, 4	
	3. A11170707A	C.	3, 4, 1, 5, 2	
	4. H17170171H	D.	3, 5, 1, 2, 4	
	5. A11710177A			
25.	1. R26794821S	A.	3, 2, 4, 1, 5	25.___
	2. O26794821T	B.	3, 4, 2, 1, 5	
	3. M26794827Z	C.	4, 2, 1, 3, 5	
	4. Q26794821R	D.	5, 4, 1, 2, 3	
	5. S26794821P			

KEY (CORRECT ANSWERS)

1.	A	11.	C
2.	D	12.	B
3.	B	13.	B
4.	C	14.	D
5.	A	15.	A
6.	C	16.	C
7.	D	17.	A
8.	B	18.	B
9.	A	19.	D
10.	D	20.	C

21. A
22. B
23. A
24. D
25. A

TEST 2

DIRECTIONS: Questions 1 through 5 consist of a set of letters and numbers located under Column I. For each question, pick the answer (A, B, C, or D) located under Column II which contains *ONLY* letters and numbers that appear in the question in Column 1. *PRINT THE LETTER OF THE CORRECT ANSWER IN THE SPACE AT THE RIGHT.*

SAMPLE QUESTION

Column I

B-9-P-H-2-Z-N-8-4-M

Column II

A. B-4-C-3-R-9
B. 4-H-P-8-6-N
C. P-2-Z-8-M-9
D. 4-B-N-5-E-Z

Choice C is the correct answer because P,2,Z,8,M and 9 all appear in the sample question. All the other choices have at least one letter or number that is not in the question.

Column I

1. 1-7-6-J-L-T-3-S-A-2

2. C-0-Q-5-3-9-H-L-2-7

3. P-3-B-C-5-6-0-E-1-T

4. U-T-Z-2-4-S-8-6-B-3

5. 4-D-F-G-C-6-8-3-J-L

Column I

1.
A. J-3-S-A-7-L
B. T-S-A-2-6-5
C. 3-7-J-L-S-Z
D. A-7-4-J-L-1

2.
A. 5-9-T-2-7-Q
B. 3-0-6-9-L-C
C. 9-L-7-Q-C-3
D. H-Q-4-5-9-7

3.
A. B-4-6-1-3-T
B. T-B-P-3-E-0
C. 5-3-0-E-B-G
D. 0-6-P-T-9-B

4.
A. 2-4-S-V-Z-3
B. B-Z-S-8-3-6
C. 4-T-U-8-L-B
D. 8-3-T-Z-1-2

5.
A. T-D-6-8-4-J
B. C-4-3-2-J-F
C. 8-3-C-5-G-6
D. C-8-6-J-G-L

1.___

2.___

3.___

4.___

5.___

Questions 6 - 12.

DIRECTIONS: Each of the questions numbered 6 through 12 consists of a long series of letters and numbers under Column I and four short series of letters and numbers under Column II. For each question, choose the short series of letters and numbers which is entirely and exactly the same as some part of the long series.

SAMPLE QUESTION:

Column I

JG13572XY89WB14

Column II

A. 1372Y8
B. XYWB14
C. 72XY89
D. J13572

In each of choices A, B, and D, one or more of the letters and numbers in the series in Column I is omitted. Only option C reproduces a segment of the series entirely and exactly. Therefore, C is the CORRECT answer to the sample question.

6. IE227FE383L4700
   A. E27FE3
   B. EF838L
   C. EL4700
   D. 83L470

7. 77J646G54NPB318
   A. NPB318
   B. J646J5
   C. 4G54NP
   D. C54NPB

8. 85887T358W24A93
   A. 858887
   B. W24A93
   C. 858W24
   D. 87T353

9. E104RY796B33H14
   A. 04RY79
   B. E14RYR
   C. 96B3H1
   D. RY7996

10. W58NP12141DE07M
    A. 8MP121
    B. W58NP1
    C. 14DEO7
    D. 12141D

11. P473R365M442V5W
    A. P47365
    B. 73P365
    C. 365M44
    D. 5X42V5

12. 865CG441V21SS59   A. 1V12SS   12.____
                     B. V21SS5
                     C. 5GC441
                     D. 894CG4

KEY (CORRECT ANSWERS)

1. A   7. A
2. C   8. B
3. B   9. A
4. B   10. D
5. D   11. C
6. D   12. B

TEST 3

DIRECTIONS: Each question from 1 to 8 consists of a set of letters and numbers. For each question, pick as your answer from the column to the right, the choice which has ONLY numbers and letters that are in the question you are answering.

To help you understand what to do, the following sample question is given:

SAMPLE: B-9-P-H-2-Z-N-8-4-M

     A. B-4-C-3-E-9
     B. 4-H-P-8-6-N
     C. P-2-Z-8-M-9
     D. 4-B-N-5-E-2

Choice C is the correct answer because P, 2, Z, 8, M, 9 are in the sample question. All the other choices have at least one letter or number that is not in the question.

Questions 1 through 4 are based on Column I.

Column I

1. X-8-3-I-H-9-4-G-P-U   A. I-G-W-8-2-1   1.____
2. 4-1-2-X-U-B-9-H-7-3   B. U-3-G-9-P-8   2.____
3. U-I-G-2-5-4-W-P-3-B   C. 3-G-I-4-S-U   3.____
4. 3-H-7-G-4-5-I-U-8   D. 9-X-4-7-2-H   4.____

Questions 5 through 8 are based on Column II.

Column II

5. L-2-9-Z-R-8-Q-Y-5-7   A. 8-R-N-3-T-Z   5.____
6. J-L-9-N-Y-8-5-Q-Z-2   B. 2-L-R-5-7-Q   6.____
7. T-Y-3-3-J-Q-2-N-R-Z   C. J-2-8-Z-Y-5   7.____
8. 8-Z-7-T-N-L-1-E-R-3   D. Z-8-9-3-L-5   8.____

KEY (CORRECT ANSWERS)

1. B
2. D
3. C
4. C
5. B
6. C
7. A
8. A

TEST 4

DIRECTIONS: Questions 1 through 5 have lines of letters and numbers. Each letter should be matched with its number in accordance with the following table:

Letter	F	R	C	A	W	L	E	N	B	T
Matching Number	0	1	2	3	4	5	6	7	8	9

From the table you can determine that the letter F has the matching number 0 below it, the letter R has the matching number 1 below it, etc.

For each question, compare each line of letters and numbers carefully to see if each letter has its correct matching number. If all the letters and numbers are matched correctly in

    none of the lines of the question, mark your answer A
    only *one* of the lines of the question, mark your answer B
    only *two* of the lines of the question, mark your answer C
    all three lines of the question, mark your answer D

    WBCR   4826
    TLBF   9580
    ATNE   3986

There is a mistake in the first line because the letter R should have its matching number 1 instead of the number 6. The second line is correct because each letter shown has the correct matching number.
There is a mistake in the third line because the letter N should have the matching number 7 instead of the number 8. Since all the letters and numbers are matched correctly in only one of the lines in the sample, the correct answer is B.

1.   EBCT   6829   1.____
    ATWR   3961
    NLBW   7584

2.   RNCT   1729   2.____
    LNCR   5728
    WAEB   5368

3.   STWB   7948   3.____
    RABL   1385
    TAEF   9360

4.   LWRB   5417   4.____
    RLWN   1647
    CBWA   2843

5.   ABTC   3792
    WCER   5261
    AWCN   3417

KEY (CORRECT ANSWERS)

1. C
2. B
3. D
4. B
5. A

TEST 5

DIRECTIONS: Assume that each of the capital letters in the table below represents the name of an employee enrolled in the city employees retirement system. The number directly beneath the letter represents the agency for which the employee works, and the small letter directly beneath represents the code for the employees account.

Name of Employee	L	O	T	Q	A	M	R	N	C
Agency	3	4	5	9	8	7	2	1	6
Account Code	r	f	b	i	d	t	g	e	n

In each of the following Questions 1 through 10, the agency code numbers and the account code letters in Columns 2 and 3 should correspond to the capital letters in Column 1 and should be in the same consecutive order. For each question, look at each column carefully and mark your answer as follows:

If there are one or more errors in *Column 2 only,* mark your answer A,
If there are one or more errors in *Column 3 only,* mark your answer B.
If there are one or more errors in Column 2 *and* one or more errors in Column 3, mark your answer C.
If there are *NO* errors in either column, mark your answer D,

The following sample question is given to help you understand the procedure.

Column 1	Column 2	Column 3
T Q L M O C	5 8 3 7 4 6	b i r t f n

In Column 2, the second agency code number (corresponding to letter Q) should be "9", not "8". Column 3 is coded correctly to Column 1. Since there is an error only in Column 2, the correct answer is A.

	Column 1	Column 2	Column 3	
1.	Q L N R C A	9 3 1 2 6 8	i f e g n d	1.____
2.	N R M O T C	1 2 7 5 4 6	e g f t b n	2.____
3.	R C T A L M	2 6 5 8 3 7	g n d b r t	3.____
4.	T A M L O N	5 7 8 3 4 1	b d t r f e	4.____
5.	A N T O R M	8 1 5 4 2 7	d e b i g t	5.____
6.	M R A L O N	7 2 8 3 4 1	t g d r f e	6.____
7.	C T N Q R O	6 5 7 9 2 4	n d e i g f	7.____
8.	Q M R O T A	9 7 2 4 5 8	i t g f b d	8.____
9.	R Q M C O L	2 9 7 4 6 3	g i t n f r	9.____
10.	N O M R T Q	1 4 7 2 5 9	e f t g b i	10.____

KEY (CORRECT ANSWERS)

1. D
2. C
3. B
4. A
5. B

6. D
7. C
8. D
9. A
10. D

TEST 6

DIRECTIONS: Each of Questions 1 through 6 consists of three lines of code letters and numbers. The numbers on each line should correspond to the code letters on the same line in accordance with the table below.

Code Letter	D	Y	K	L	P	U	S	R	A	E
Corresponding Number	0	1	2	3	4	5	6	7	8	9

On some of the lines an error exists in the coding. Compare the letters and numbers in each question carefully. If you find an error or errors on
 only *one* of the lines in the question, mark your answer A;
 any *two* lines in the question, mark your answer B;
 all *three* lines in the question, mark your answer C;
 none of the lines in the question, mark your answer D.

SAMPLE QUESTION
KSRYELD - 2671930
SAPUEKL - 6845913
RYKADLP - 5128034

In the above sample, the first line is correct since each code letter listed has the correct corresponding number. On the second line, an error exists because code letter K should have number 2 instead of number 1. On the third line, an error exists because the code letter R should have the number 7 instead of the number 5. Since there are errors on two of the three lines, the correct answer is B.

Now answer the following questions, using the same procedure.

1. YPUSRLD - 1456730
   UPSAEDY - 5648901
   PREYDKS - 4791026   1. D

2. AERLPUS - 8973456
   DKLYDPA - 0231048
   UKLDREP - 5230794   2. D

3. DAPUSLA - 0845683
   YKLDLPS - 1230356
   PUSKYDE - 4562101   3. C

4. LRPUPDL - 3745403
   SUPLEDR - 6543907
   PKEYDLU - 4291025   4. A

5. KEYDESR - 2910967
   PRSALEY - 4678391
   LSRAYSK - 3687162   5. A

6. YESREYL - 1967913
   PLPRAKY - 4346821
   YLPSRDU - 1346705   6. A

KEY (CORRECT ANSWERS)

1. A
2. D
3. C
4. A
5. B
6. A

READING COMPREHENSION
UNDERSTANDING AND INTERPRETING WRITTEN MATERIAL
EXAMINATION SECTION
TEST 1

DIRECTIONS: Each question or incomplete statement is followed by several suggested answers or completions. Select the one that BEST answers the question or completes the statement. *PRINT THE LETTER OF THE CORRECT ANSWER IN THE SPACE AT THE RIGHT.*

Questions 1-3.

DIRECTIONS: Questions 1 through 3 are to be answered SOLELY on the basis of the following statement.

The equipment in a mailroom may include a mail metering machine. This machine simultaneously stamps, postmarks, seals, and counts letters as fast as the operator can feed them. It can also print the proper postage directly on a gummed strip to be affixed to bulky items. It is equipped with a meter which is removed from the machine and sent to the postmaster to be set for a given number of stampings of any denomination. The setting of the meter must be paid for in advance. One of the advantages of metered mail is that it by-passes the cancellation operation and thereby facilitates handling by the post office. Mail metering also makes the pilfering of stamps impossible, but does not prevent the passage of personal mail in company envelopes through the meters unless there is established a rigid control or censorship over outgoing mail.

1. According to this statement, the postmaster

   A. is responsible for training new clerks in the use of mail metering machines
   B. usually recommends that both large and small firms adopt the use of mail metering machines
   C. is responsible for setting the meter to print a fixed number of stampings
   D. examines the mail metering machine to see that they are properly installed in the mailroom

1._____

2. According to this statement, the use of mail metering machines

   A. requires the employment of more clerks in a mailroom than does the use of postage stamps
   B. interferes with the handling of large quantities of outgoing mail
   C. does not prevent employees from sending their personal letters at company expense
   D. usually involves smaller expenditures for mailroom equipment than does the use of postage stamps

2._____

3. On the basis of this statement, it is MOST accurate to state that

   A. mail metering machines are often used for opening envelopes
   B. postage stamps are generally used when bulky packages are to be mailed
   C. the use of metered mail tends to interfere with rapid mail handling by the post office
   D. mail metering machines can seal and count letters at the same time

3._____

Questions 4-5.

DIRECTIONS: Questions 4 and 5 are to be answered SOLELY on the basis of the following statement.

Forms are printed sheets of paper on which information is to be entered. While what is printed on the form is most important, the kind of paper used in making the form is also important. The kind of paper should be selected with regard to the use to which the form will be subjected. Printing a form on an unnecessarily expensive grade of papers is wasteful. On the other hand, using too cheap or flimsy a form can materially interfere with satisfactory performance of the work the form is being planned to do. Thus, a form printed on both sides normally requires a heavier paper than a form printed only on one side. Forms to be used as permanent records, or which are expected to have a very long life in files, requires a quality of paper which will not disintegrate or discolor with age. A form which will go through a great deal of handling requires a strong tough paper, while thinness is a necessary qualification where the making of several carbon copies of a form will be require

4. According to this statement, the type of paper used for making forms 4.___

    A. should be chosen in accordance with the use to which the form will be put
    B. should be chosen before the type of printing to be used has been decided upon
    C. is as important as the information which is printed on it
    D. should be strong enough to be used for any purpose

5. According to this statement, forms that are 5.___

    A. printed on both sides are usually economical and desirable
    B. to be filed permanently should not deteriorate as time goes on
    C. expected to last for a long time should be handled carefully
    D. to be filed should not be printed on inexpensive paper

Questions 6-8.

DIRECTIONS: Questions 6 through 8 are to be answered SOLELY on the basis of the following paragraph.

The increase in the number of public documents in the last two centuries closely matches the increase in population in the United States. The great number of public documents has become a serious threat to their usefulness. It is necessary to have programs which will reduce the number of public documents that are kept and which will, at the same time, assure keeping those that have value. Such programs need a great deal of thought to have any success.

6. According to the above paragraph, public documents may be LESS useful if 6.___

    A. the files are open to the public
    B. the record room is too small
    C. the copying machine is operated only during normal working hours
    D. too many records are being kept

7. According to the above paragraph, the growth of the population in the United States has matched the growth in the quantity of public documents for a period of MOST NEARLY _____ years.

   A. 50   B. 100   C. 200   D. 300

8. According to the above paragraph, the increased number of public documents has made it necessary to

   A. find out which public documents are worth keeping
   B. reduce the great number of public documents by decreasing government services
   C. eliminate the copying of all original public documents
   D. avoid all new copying devices

Questions 9-10.

DIRECTIONS: Questions 9 and 10 are to be answered SOLELY on the basis of the following paragraph.

The work goals of an agency can best be reached if the employees understand and agree with these goals. One way to gain such understanding and agreement is for management to encourage and seriously consider suggestions from employees in the setting of agency goals.

9. On the basis of the above paragraph, the BEST way to achieve the work goals of an agency is to

   A. make certain that employees work as hard as possible
   B. study the organizational structure of the agency
   C. encourage employees to think seriously about the agency's problems
   D. stimulate employee understanding of the work goals.

10. On the basis of the above paragraph, understanding and agreement with agency goals can be gained by

    A. allowing the employees to set agency goals
    B. reaching agency goals quickly
    C. legislative review of agency operations
    D. employee participation in setting agency goals

Questions 11-13.

DIRECTIONS: Questions 11 through 13 are to be answered SOLELY on the basis of the following paragraph.

In order to organize records properly, it is necessary to start from their very beginning and trace each copy of the record to find out how it is used, how long it is used, and what may finally be done with it. Although several copies of the record are made, one copy should be marked as the copy of record. This is the formal legal copy, held to meet the requirements of the law. The other copies may be retained for brief periods for reference purposes, but these copies should not be kept after their usefulness as reference ends. There is another reason for tracing records through the office and that is to determine how long it takes the copy of record to reach the central file. The copy of record must not be kept longer than necessary by the section of the office which has prepared it, but should be sent to the central file as soon as possible so that it can be available to the various sections of the office. The central file can make the copy of record available to the various sections of the office at an early date only if it arrives at the central file as quickly as possible. Just as soon as its immediate or active service period is ended, the copy of record should be removed from the central file and put into the inactive file in the office to be stored for whatever length of time may be necessary to meet legal requirements, and then destroyed.

11. According to the above paragraph, a reason for tracing records through an office is to

    A. determine how long the central file must keep the records
    B. organize records properly
    C. find out how many copies of each record are required
    D. identify the copy of record

12. According to the above paragraph, in order for the central file to have the copy of record available as soon as possible for the various sections of the office, it is MOST important that the

    A. copy of record to be sent to the central file meets the requirements of the law
    B. copy of record is not kept in the inactive file too long
    C. section preparing the copy of record does not unduly delay in sending it to the central file
    D. central file does not keep the copy of record beyond its active service period

13. According to the above paragraph, the length of time a copy of a record is kept in the inactive file of an office depends CHIEFLY on the

    A. requirements of the law
    B. length of time that is required to trace the copy of record through the office
    C. use that is made of the copy of record
    D. length of the period that the copy of record is used for reference purposes

Questions 14-16.

DIRECTIONS: Questions 14 through 16 are to be answered SOLELY on the basis of the following paragraph.

The office was once considered as nothing more than a focal point of internal and external correspondence. It was capable only of dispatching a few letters upon occasion and of preparing records of little practical value. Under such a concept, the vitality of the office force was impaired. Initiative became stagnant, and the lot of the office worker was not likely to be a happy on However, under the new concept of office management, the possibilities of waste and mismanagement in office operation are now fully recognized, as are the possibilities for the modern office to assist in the direction and control of business operations. Fortunately, the modern concept of the office as a centralized service-rendering unit is gaining ever greater acceptance in today's complex business world, for without the modern office, the production wheels do not turn and the distribution of goods and services is not possibl. I

14. According to the above paragraph, the fundamental difference between the old and the new concept of the office is the change in the   14.____

    A. accepted functions of the office
    B. content and the value of the records kept
    C. office methods and systems
    D. vitality and morale of the office force

15. According to the above paragraph, an office operated today under the old concept of the office MOST likely would   15.____

    A. make older workers happy in their jobs
    B. be part of an old thriving business concern
    C. have a passive role in the conduct of a business enterprise
    D. attract workers who do not believe in modern methods

16. Of the following, the MOST important implication of the above paragraph is that a present day business organization cannot function effectively without the   16.____

    A. use of modern office equipment
    B. participation and cooperation of the office
    C. continued modernization of office procedures
    D. employment of office workers with skill and initiative

Questions 17-20.

DIRECTIONS: Questions 17 through 20 are to be answered SOLELY on the basis of the following paragraph.

   A report is frequently ineffective because the person writing it is not fully acquainted with all the necessary details before he actually starts to construct the report. All details pertaining to the subject should be known before the report is started. If the essential facts are not known, they should be investigate It is wise to have essential facts written down rather than to depend too much on memory, especially if the facts pertain to such matters as amounts, dates, names of persons, or other specific data. When the necessary information has been gathered, the general plan and content of the report should be thought out before the writing is actually begun. A person with little or no experience in writing reports may find that it is wise to make a brief outline. Persons with more experience should not need a written outline, but they should make mental notes of the steps they are to follow. If writing reports without dictation is a regular part of an office worker's duties, he should set aside a certain time during the day when he is least likely to be interrupted. That may be difficult, but in most offices there are certain times in the day when the callers, telephone calls, and other interruptions are not numerous. During those times, it is best to write reports that need undivided concentration. Reports that are written amid a series of interruptions may be poorly don

17. Before starting to write an effective report, it is necessary to   17.____

    A. memorize all specific information
    B. disregard ambiguous data
    C. know all pertinent information
    D. develop a general plan

18. Reports dealing with complex and difficult material should be

    A. prepared and written by the supervisor of the unit
    B. written when there is the least chance of interruption
    C. prepared and written as part of regular office routine
    D. outlined and then dictated

19. According to the paragraph, employees with no prior familiarity in writing reports may find it helpful to

    A. prepare a brief outline
    B. mentally prepare a synopsis of the report's content
    C. have a fellow employee help in writing the report
    D. consult previous reports

20. In writing a report, needed information which is unclear should be

    A. disregarded   B. memorized
    C. investigated   D. gathered

Questions 21-25.

DIRECTIONS: Questions 21 through 25 are to be answered SOLELY on the basis of the following passage.

Positive discipline minimizes the amount of personal supervision required and aids in the maintenance of standards. When a new employee has been properly introduced and carefully instructed, when he has come to know the supervisor and has confidence in the supervisor's ability to take care of him, when he willingly cooperates with the supervisor, that employee has been under positive discipline and can be put on his own to produce the quantity and quality of work desire Negative discipline, the fear of transfer to a less desirable location, for example, to a limited extent may restrain certain individuals from overt violation of rules and regulations governing attendance and conduct which in governmental agencies are usually on at least an agency-wide basis. Negative discipline may prompt employees to perform according to certain rules to avoid a penalty such as, for example, docking for tardiness.

21. According to the above passage, it is reasonable to assume that in the area of discipline, the first-line supervisor in a governmental agency has GREATER scope for action in

    A. *positive* discipline, because negative discipline is largely taken care of by agency rules and regulations
    B. *negative* discipline, because rules and procedures are already fixed and the supervisor can rely on them
    C. *positive* discipline, because the supervisor is in a position to recommend transfers
    D. *negative* discipline, because positive discipline is reserved for people on a higher supervisory level

22. In order to maintain positive discipline of employees under his supervision, it is MOST important for a supervisor to

    A. assure each employee that he has nothing to worry about
    B. insist at the outset on complete cooperation from employees

C. be sure that each employee is well trained in his job
D. inform new employees of the penalties for not meeting standards

23. According to the above passage, a feature of negative discipline is that it

    A. may lower employee morale
    B. may restrain employees from disobeying the rules
    C. censures equal treatment of employees
    D. tends to create standards for quality of work

24. A REASONABLE conclusion based on the above passage is that positive discipline benefits a supervisor because

    A. he can turn over orientation and supervision of a new employee to one of his subordinates
    B. subordinates learn to cooperate with one another when working on an assignment
    C. it is easier to administer
    D. it cuts down, in the long run, on the amount of time the supervisor needs to spend on direct supervision

25. Based on the above passage, it is REASONABLE to assume, that an important difference between positive discipline and negative discipline is that positive discipline

    A. is concerned with the quality of work and negative discipline with the quantity of work
    B. leads to a more desirable basis for motivation of the employee
    C. is more likely to be concerned with agency rules and regulations
    D. uses fear while negative discipline uses penalties to prod employees to adequate performance

KEY (CORRECT ANSWERS)

1. C
2. C
3. D
4. A
5. B

6. D
7. C
8. A
9. D
10. D

11. B
12. C
13. A
14. A
15. C

16. B
17. C
18. B
19. A
20. B

21. A
22. C
23. B
24. D
25. B

TEST 2

Questions 1-6.

DIRECTIONS: Questions 1 through 6 are to be answered SOLELY on the basis of the following passage.

Inherent in all organized endeavors is the need to resolve the individual differences involved in conflict. Conflict may be either a positive or negative factor since it may lead to creativity, innovation and progress on the one hand, or it may result, on the other hand, in a deterioration or even destruction of the organization. Thus, some forms of conflict are desirable, whereas others are undesirable and ethically wrong.

There are three management strategies which deal with interpersonal conflict. In the, *divide-and-rule strategy,* management attempts to maintain control by limiting the conflict to those directly involved and preventing their disagreement from spreading to the larger group. The *suppression-of-differences strategy* entails ignoring conflicts or pretending they are irrelevant. In the *working-through-differences strategy,* management actively attempts to solve or resolve intergroup or interpersonal conflicts. Of the three strategies, only the last directly attacks and has the potential for eliminating the causes of conflict. An essential part of this strategy, however, is its employment by a committed and relatively mature management team.

1. According to the above passage, the *divide-and-rule strategy tor* dealing with conflict is the attempt to

    A. involve other people in the conflict
    B. restrict the conflict to those participating in it
    C. divide the conflict into positive and negative factors
    D. divide the conflict into a number of smaller ones

2. The word *conflict* is used in relation to both positive and negative factors in this passage. Which one of the following words is MOST likely to describe the activity which the word *conflict,* in the sense of the passage, implies?

    A. Competition   B. Confusion
    C. Cooperation   D. Aggression

3. According to the above passage, which one of the following characteristics is shared by both the *suppression-of-differences strategy* and the *divide-and-rule strategy*?

    A. Pretending that conflicts are irrelevant
    B. Preventing conflicts from spreading to the group situation
    C. Failure to directly attack the causes of conflict
    D. Actively attempting to resolve interpersonal conflict

4. According to the above passage, the successful resolution of interpersonal conflict requires

    A. allowing the group to mediate conflicts between two individuals
    B. division of the conflict into positive and negative factors
    C. involvement of a committed, mature management team
    D. ignoring minor conflicts until they threaten the organization

1.___

2.___

3.___

4.___

5. Which can be MOST reasonably inferred from the above passage? conflict between two individuals is LEAST likely to continue when management uses

   A. the *working-through differences strategy*
   B. the *suppression-of differences strategy*
   C. the *divide-and-rule strategy*
   D. a combination of all three strategies

6. According to the above passage, a DESIRABLE result of conflict in an organization is when conflict

   A. exposes production problems in the organization
   B. can be easily ignored by management
   C. results in advancement of more efficient managers
   D. leads to development of new methods

Questions 7-13.

DIRECTIONS: Questions 7 through 13 are to be answered SOLELY on the basis of the passage below.

Modern management places great emphasis on the concept of communication. The communication process consists of the steps through which an idea or concept passes from its inception by one person, the sender, until it is acted upon by another person, the receiver. Through an understanding of these steps and some of the possible barriers that may occur, more effective communication may be achieve The first step in the communication process is ideation by the sender. This is the formation of the intended content of the message he wants to transmit. In the next step, encoding, the sender organizes his ideas into a series of symbols designed to communicate his message to his intended receiver. He selects suitable words or phrases that can be understood by the receiver, and he also selects the appropriate media to be used-for example, memorandum, conference, etc. The third step is transmission of the encoded message through selected channels in the organizational structure. In the fourth step, the receiver enters the process by tuning in to receive the message. If the receiver does not function, however, the message is lost. For example, if the message is oral, the receiver must be a good listener. The fifth step is decoding of the message by the receiver, as for example, by changing words into ideas. At this step, the decoded message may not be the same idea that the sender originally encoded because the sender and receiver have different perceptions regarding the meaning of certain words. Finally, the receiver acts or responds. He may file the information, ask for more information, or take other action. There can be no assurance, however, that communication has taken place unless there is some type of feedback to the sender in the form of an acknowledgement that the message was received.

7. According to the above passage, *ideation* is the process by which the

   A. sender develops the intended content of the message
   B. sender organizes his ideas into a series of symbols
   C. receiver tunes in to receive the message
   D. receiver decodes the message

8. In the last sentence of the passage, the word *feedback* refers to the process by which the sender is assured that the

    A. receiver filed the information
    B. receiver's perception is the same as his own
    C. message was received
    D. message was properly interpreted

9. Which one of the following BEST shows the order of the steps in the communication process as described in the passage?

    A. 1 - ideation   2 - encoding
        3 - decoding   4 - transmission
        5 - receiving   6 - action
        7 - feedback to the sender

    B. 1 - ideation   2 - encoding
        3 - transmission   4 - decoding
        5 - receiving   6 - action
        7 - feedback to the sender

    C. 1 - ideation   2 - decoding
        3 - transmission   4 - receiving
        5 - encoding   6 - action
        7 - feedback to the sender

    D. 1 - ideation   2 - encoding
        3 - transmission   4 - receiving
        5 - decoding   6 - action
        7 - feedback to the sender

10. Which one of the following BEST expresses the main theme of the passage?

    A. Different individuals have the same perceptions regarding the meaning of words.
    B. An understanding of the steps in the communication process may achieve better communication.
    C. Receivers play a passive role in the communication process.
    D. Senders should not communicate with receivers who transmit feedback.

11. The above passage implies that a receiver does NOT function properly when he

    A. transmits feedback   B. files the information
    C. is a poor listener   D. asks for more information

12. Which one of the following, according to the above passage, is included in the SECOND step of the communication process?

    A. Selecting the appropriate media to be used in transmission
    B. Formulation of the intended content of the message
    C. Using appropriate media to respond to the receiver's feedback
    D. Transmitting the message through selected channels in the organization

13. The above passage implies that the *decoding process* is MOST NEARLY the reverse of the _____ process.

    A. transmission   B. receiving
    C. feedback   D. encoding

Questions 14-19.

DIRECTIONS: Questions 14 through 19 are to be answered SOLELY on the basis of the following passage.

It is often said that no system will work if the people who carry it out do not want it to work. In too many cases, a departmental reorganization that seemed technically sound and economically practical has proved to be a failure because the planners neglected to take the human factor into account. The truth is that employees are likely to feel threatened when they learn that a major change is in the win It does not matter whether or not the change actually poses a threat to an employee; the fact that he believes it does or fears it might is enough to make him feel insecure. Among the dangers he fears, the foremost is the possibility that his job may cease to exist and that he may be laid off or shunted into a less skilled position at lower pay. Even if he knows that his own job category is secure, however, he is likely to fear losing some of the important intangible advantages of his present position-for instance, he may fear that he will be separated from his present companions and thrust in with a group of strangers, or that he will find himself in a lower position on the organizational ladder if a new position is created above his.

It is important that management recognize these natural fears and take them into account in planning any kind of major change. While there is no cut-and-dried formula for preventing employee resistance, there are several steps that can be taken to reduce employees' fears and gain their cooperation. First, unwarranted fears can be dispelled if employees are kept informed of the planning from the start and if they know exactly what to expect. Next, assurance on matters such as retraining, transfers, and placement help should be given as soon as it is clear what direction the reorganization will take. Finally, employees' participation in the planning should be actively sought. There is a great psychological difference between feeling that a change is being forced upon one from the outside, and feeling that one is an insider who is helping to bring about a change.

14. According to the above passage, employees who are not in real danger of losing their jobs because of a proposed reorganization   14.____

    A. will be eager to assist in the reorganization
    B. will pay little attention to the reorganization
    C. should not be taken into account in planning the reorganization
    D. are nonetheless likely to feel threatened by the reorganization

15. The passage mentions the *intangible advantages* of a position.   15.____
    Which of the following BEST describes the kind of advantages alluded to in the passage?

    A. Benefits such as paid holidays and vacations
    B. Satisfaction of human needs for things like friendship and status
    C. Qualities such as leadership and responsibility
    D. A work environment that meets satisfactory standards of health and safety

16. According to the passage, an employee's fear that a reorganization may separate him from his present companions is a (n)   16.____

    A. childish and immature reaction to change
    B. unrealistic feeling since this is not going to happen

C. possible reaction that the planners should be aware of
D. incentive to employees to participate in the planning

17. On the basis of the above passage, it would be DESIRABLE, when planning a departmental reorganization, to

    A. be governed by employee feelings and attitudes
    B. give some employees lower positions
    C. keep employees informed
    D. lay off those who are less skilled

18. What does the passage say can be done to help gain employees' cooperation in a reorganization?

    A. Making sure that the change is technically sound, that it is economically practical, and that the human factor is taken into account
    B. Keeping employees fully informed, offering help in fitting them into new positions, and seeking their participation in the planning
    C. Assuring employees that they will not be laid off, that they will not be reassigned to a group of strangers, and that no new positions will be created on the organization ladder
    D. Reducing employees' fears, arranging a retraining program, and providing for transfers

19. Which of the following suggested titles would be MOST appropriate for this passage?

    A. PLANNING A DEPARTMENTAL REORGANIZATION
    B. WHY EMPLOYEES ARE AFRAID
    C. LOOKING AHEAD TO THE FUTURE
    D. PLANNING FOR CHANGE: THE HUMAN FACTOR

Questions 20-22.

DIRECTIONS: Questions 20 through 22 are to be answered SOLELY on the basis of the following passage.

The achievement of good human relations is essential if a business office is to produce at top efficiency and is to be a pleasant place in which to work. All office workers plan an important role in handling problems in human relations. They should, therefore, strive to acquire the understanding, tactfulness, and awareness necessary to deal effectively with actual office situations involving co-workers on all levels. Only in this way can they truly become responsible, interested, cooperative, and helpful members of the staff.

20. The selection implies that the MOST important value of good human relations in an office is to develop

    A. efficiency   B. cooperativeness
    C. tact   D. pleasantness and efficiency

21. Office workers should acquire understanding in dealing with

    A. co-workers   B. subordinates
    C. superiors   D. all members of the staff

22. The selection indicates that a highly competent secretary who is also very argumentative is meeting office requirements   22.____

    A. wholly   B. partly
    C. slightly   D. not at all

Questions 23-25.

DIRECTIONS: Questions 23 through 25 are to be answered SOLELY on the basis of the following passage.

It is common knowledge that ability to do a particular job and performance on the job do not always go hand in hand. Persons with great potential abilities sometimes fall down on the job because of laziness or lack of interest in the job, while persons with mediocre talents have often achieved excellent results through their industry and their loyalty to the interests of their employers. It is clear; therefore, that in a balanced personnel program, measures of employee ability need to be supplemented by measures of employee performance, for the final test of any employee is his performance on the job.

23. The MOST accurate of the following statements, on the basis of the above paragraph, is that   23.____

    A. employees who lack ability are usually not industrious
    B. an employee's attitudes are more important than his abilities
    C. mediocre employees who are interested in their work are preferable to employees who possess great ability
    D. superior capacity for performance should be supplemented with proper attitudes

24. On the basis of the above paragraph, the employee of most value to his employer is NOT necessarily the one who   24.____

    A. best understands the significance of his duties
    B. achieves excellent results
    C. possesses the greatest talents
    D. produces the greatest amount of work

25. According to the above paragraph, an employee's efficiency is BEST determined by an   25.____

    A. appraisal of his interest in his work
    B. evaluation of the work performed by him
    C. appraisal of his loyalty to his employer
    D. evaluation of his potential ability to perform his work

KEY (CORRECT ANSWERS)

1. B
2. A
3. C
4. C
5. A

6. D
7. A
8. C
9. D
10. B

11. C
12. A
13. D
14. D
15. B

16. C
17. C
18. B
19. D
20. D

21. D
22. B
23. D
24. C
25. B

TEST 3

Questions 1-8.

DIRECTIONS: Questions 1 through 8 are to be answered SOLELY on the basis of the following information and directions.

Assume that you are a clerk in a city agency. Your supervisor has asked you to classify each of the accidents that happened to employees in the agency into the following five categories:

    A. An accident that occurred in the period from January through June, between 9 M. and 12 Noon, that was the result of carelessness on the part of the injured employee, that caused the employee to lose less than seven working hours, that happened to an employee who was 40 years of age or over, and who was employed in the agency for less than three years;

    B. An accident that occurred in the period from July through December, after 1 P.M., that was the result of unsafe conditions, that caused the injured employee to lose less than seven working hours, that happened to an employee who was 40 years of age or over, and who was employed in the agency for three years or more;

    C. An accident that occurred in the period from January through June, after 1 P.M., that was the result of carelessness on the part of the injured employee, that caused the injured employee to lose seven or more working hours, that happened to an employee who was less than 40 years old, and who was employed in the agency for three years or more;

    D. An accident that occurred in the period from July through December, between 9 M. and 12 Noon, that was the result of unsafe conditions, that caused the injured employee to lose seven or more working hours, that happened to an employee who was less than 40 years old, and who was employed in the agency for less than three years;

    E. Accidents that cannot be classified in any of the foregoing groups. NOTE: In classifying these accidents, an employee's age and length of service are computed as of the date of accident. In all cases, it is to be assumed that each employee has been employed continuously in city service, and that each employee works seven hours a day, from 9 M. to 5 P.M., with lunch from 12 Noon to 1 P.M. In each question, consider only the information which will assist you in classifying the accident. Any information which is of no assistance in classifying an accident should not be considered.

1. The unsafe condition of the stairs in the building caused Miss Perkins to have an accident on October 14, 2003 at 4 P.M. When she returned to work the following day at 1 P.M., Miss Perkins said that the accident was the first one that had occurred to her in her ten years of employment with the agency. She was born on April 27, 1962. 1.____

2. On the day after she completed her six-month probationary period of employment with the agency, Miss Green, who had been considered a careful worker by her supervisor, injured her left foot in an accident caused by her own carelessness. She went home immediately after the accident, which occurred at 10 M., March 19, 2004, but returned to work at the regular time on the following morning. Miss Green was born July 12, 1963 in New York City. 2.____

3. The unsafe condition of a duplicating machine caused Mr. Martin to injure himself in an accident on September 8, 2006 at 2 P.M. As a result of the accident, he was unable to work the remainder of the day, but returned to his office ready for work on the following morning. Mr. Martin, who has been working for the agency since April 1, 2003, was born in St. Louis on February 1, 1968.   3.___

4. Mr. Smith was hospitalized for two weeks because of a back injury resulted from an accident on the morning of November 16, 2006. Investigation of the accident revealed that it was caused by the unsafe condition of the floor on which Mr. Smith had been walking. Mr. Smith, who is an accountant, has been anemployee of the agency since March 1, 2004, and was born in Ohio on June 10, 1968.   4.___

5. Mr. Allen cut his right hand because he was careless in, operating a multilith machine. Mr. Allen, who was 33 years old when the accident took place, has been employed by the agency since August 17, 1992. The accident, which occurred on January 26, 2006, at 2 P.M., caused Mr. Allen to be absent from work for the rest of the day. He was able to return to work the next morning.   5.___

6. Mr. Rand, who is a college graduate, was born on December, 28, 1967, and has been working for the agency since January 7, 2002. On Monday, April 25, 2005, at 2 P.M., his carelessness in operating a duplicating machine caused him to have an accident and to be sent home from work immediately. Fortunately, he was able to return to work at his regular time on the following Wednesday.   6.___

7. Because he was careless in running down a flight of stairs, Mr. Brown fell, bruising his right hand. Although the accident occurred shortly after he arrived for work on the morning of May 22, 2006, he was unable to resume work until 3 P.M. that day. Mr. Brown was born on August 15, 1955, and began working for the agency on September 12, 2003, as a clerk, at a salary of $22,750 per annum.   7.___

8. On December 5, 2005, four weeks after he had begun working for the agency, the unsafe condition of an automatic stapling machine caused Mr. Thomas to injure himself in an accident. Mr. Thomas, who was born on May 19,1975, lost three working days because of the accident, which occurred at 11:45 M.   8.___

Questions 9-10.

DIRECTIONS: Questions 9 and 10 are to be answered SOLELY on the basis of the following paragraph.

An impending reorganization within an agency will mean loss by transfer of several professional staff members from the personnel division. The division chief is asked to designate the persons to be transferred. After reviewing the implications of this reduction of staff with his assistant, the division chief discusses the matter at a staff meeting. He adopts the recommendations of several staff members to have volunteers make up the required reduction.

9. The decision to permit personnel to volunteer for transfer is 9.____
   A. *poor;* it is not likely that the members of a division are of equal value to the division chief
   B. *good;* dissatisfied members will probably be more productive elsewhere
   C. *poor;* the division chief has abdicated his responsibility to carry out the order given to him
   D. *good;* morale among remaining staff is likely to improve in a more cohesive framework

10. Suppose that one of the volunteers is a recently appointed employee who has completed 10.____
    his probationary period acceptably, but whose attitude toward division operations and agency administration tends to be rather negative and sometimes even abrasive. Because of his lack of commitment to the division, his transfer is recommended. If the transfer is approved, the division chief should, prior to the transfer,
    A. discuss with the staff the importance of commitment to the work of the agency and its relationship with job satisfaction
    B. refrain from any discussion of attitude with the employee
    C. discuss with the employee his concern about the employee's attitude
    D. avoid mention of attitude in the evaluation appraisal prepared for the receiving division chief

Questions 11-16.

DIRECTIONS: Questions 11 through 16 are to be answered SOLELY on the basis of the following paragraph.

Methods of administration of office activities, much of which consists of providing information and *know-how* needed to coordinate both activities within that particular office and other offices, have been among the last to come under the spotlight of management analysis, Progress has been rapid during the past decade, however, and is now accelerating at such a pace that an *information revolution* in office management appears to be in the making. Although triggered by technological breakthroughs in electronic computers and other giant steps in mechanization, this information revolution must be attributed to underlying forces, such as the increased complexity of both governmental and private enterprise, and ever-keener competition. Size, diversification, specialization of function, and decentralization are among the forces which make coordination of activities both more imperative and more difficult. Increased competition, both domestic and international, leaves little margin for error in managerial decisions. Several developments during recent years indicate an evolving pattern. In 1960, the American Management Association expanded the scope of its activities and changed the name of its Office Management Division to Administrative Services Division. Also in 1960, the magazine *Office Management* merged with the magazine *American Business,* and this new publication was named *Administrative Management.*

4 (#3)

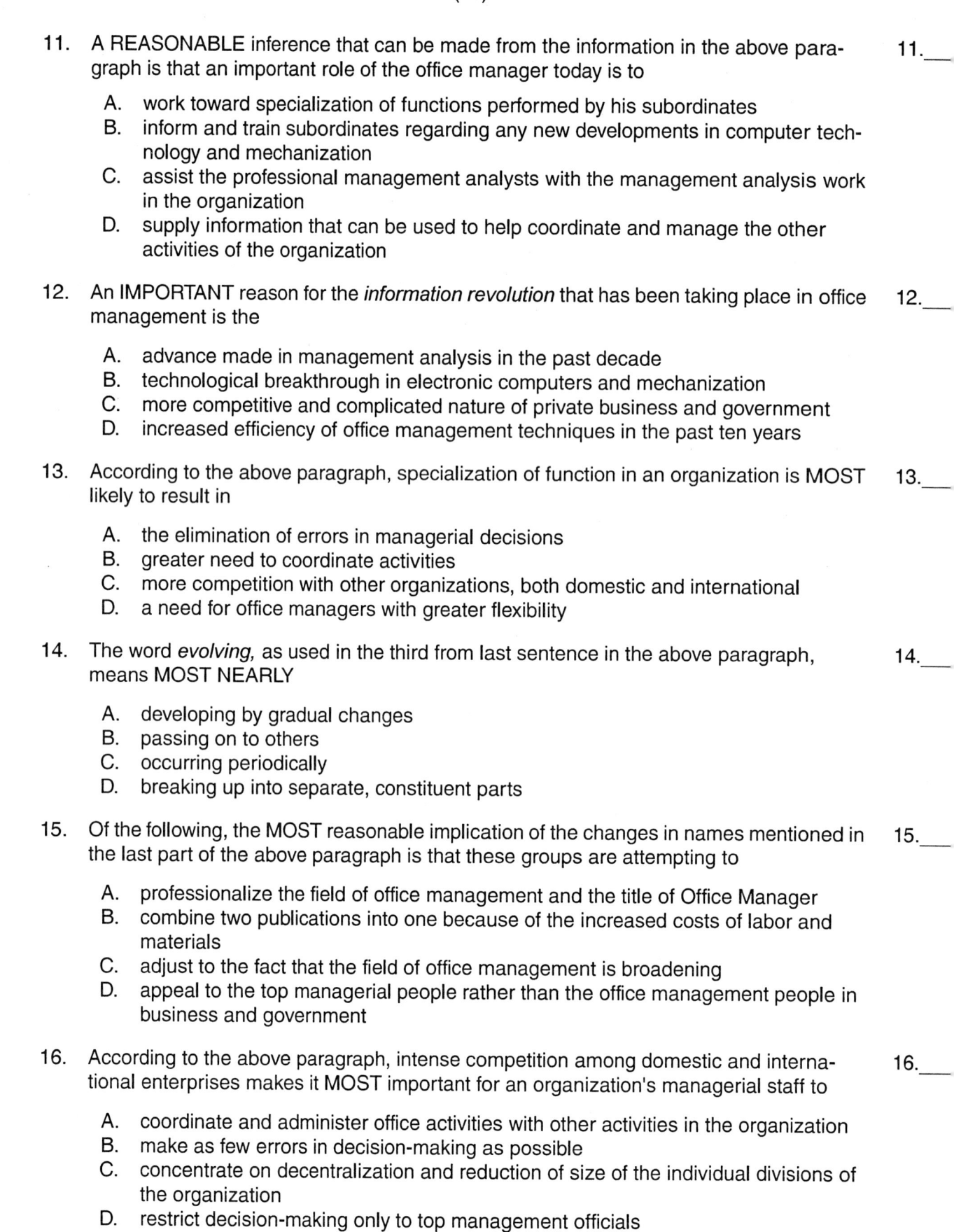

11. A REASONABLE inference that can be made from the information in the above paragraph is that an important role of the office manager today is to   11.___

    A. work toward specialization of functions performed by his subordinates
    B. inform and train subordinates regarding any new developments in computer technology and mechanization
    C. assist the professional management analysts with the management analysis work in the organization
    D. supply information that can be used to help coordinate and manage the other activities of the organization

12. An IMPORTANT reason for the *information revolution* that has been taking place in office management is the   12.___

    A. advance made in management analysis in the past decade
    B. technological breakthrough in electronic computers and mechanization
    C. more competitive and complicated nature of private business and government
    D. increased efficiency of office management techniques in the past ten years

13. According to the above paragraph, specialization of function in an organization is MOST likely to result in   13.___

    A. the elimination of errors in managerial decisions
    B. greater need to coordinate activities
    C. more competition with other organizations, both domestic and international
    D. a need for office managers with greater flexibility

14. The word *evolving,* as used in the third from last sentence in the above paragraph, means MOST NEARLY   14.___

    A. developing by gradual changes
    B. passing on to others
    C. occurring periodically
    D. breaking up into separate, constituent parts

15. Of the following, the MOST reasonable implication of the changes in names mentioned in the last part of the above paragraph is that these groups are attempting to   15.___

    A. professionalize the field of office management and the title of Office Manager
    B. combine two publications into one because of the increased costs of labor and materials
    C. adjust to the fact that the field of office management is broadening
    D. appeal to the top managerial people rather than the office management people in business and government

16. According to the above paragraph, intense competition among domestic and international enterprises makes it MOST important for an organization's managerial staff to   16.___

    A. coordinate and administer office activities with other activities in the organization
    B. make as few errors in decision-making as possible
    C. concentrate on decentralization and reduction of size of the individual divisions of the organization
    D. restrict decision-making only to top management officials

Questions 17-21.

DIRECTIONS: Questions 17 through 21 are to be answered SOLELY on the basis of the following passage.

For some office workers, it is useful to be familiar with the four main classes of domestic mail; for others, it is essential. Each class has a different rate of postage, and some have requirements concerning wrapping, sealing, or special information to be placed on the package. First class mail, the class which may not be opened for postal inspection, includes letters, postcards, business reply cards, and other kinds of written matter. There are different rates for some of the kinds of cards which can be sent by first class mail. The maximum weight for an item sent by first class mail is 70 pounds. An item which is not letter size should be marked *First Class* on all sides. Although office workers most often come into contact with first class mail, they may find it helpful to know something about the other classes. Second class mail is generally used for mailing newspapers and magazines. Publishers of these articles must meet certain U.S. Postal Service requirements in order to obtain a permit to use second class mailing rates. Third class mail, which must weigh less than 1 pound, includes printed materials and merchandise parcels. There are two rate structures for this class - a single piece rate and a bulk rat Fourth class mail, also known as parcel post, includes packages weighing from one to 40 pounds. For more information about these classes of mail and the actual mailing rates, contact your local post office.

17. According to this passage, first class mail is the *only* class which 17.____

    A. has a limit on the maximum weight of an item
    B. has different rates for items within the class
    C. may not be opened for postal inspection
    D. should be used by office workers

18. According to this passage, the one of the following items which may CORRECTLY be sent by fourth class mail is a 18.____

    A. magazine weighing one-half pound
    B. package weighing one-half pound
    C. package weighing two pounds
    D. postcard

19. According to this passage, there are different postage rates for 19.____

    A. a newspaper sent by second class mail and a magazine sent by second class mail
    B. each of the classes of mail
    C. each pound of fourth class mail
    D. printed material sent by third class mail and merchandise parcels sent by third class mail

20. In order to send a newspaper by second class mail, a publisher MUST 20.____

    A. have met certain postal requirements and obtained a permit
    B. indicate whether he wants to use the single piece or the bulk rate
    C. make certain that the newspaper weighs less than one pound
    D. mark the newspaper *Second Class* on the top and bottom of the wrapper

21. Of the following types of information, the one which is NOT mentioned in the passage is the   21.___

    A. class of mail to which parcel post belongs
    B. kinds of items which can be sent by each class of mail
    C. maximum weight for an item sent by fourth class mail
    D. postage rate for each of the four classes of mail

Questions 22-25.

DIRECTIONS: Questions 22 through 25 are to be answered SOLELY on the basis of the following paragraph.

A standard comprises characteristics attached to an aspect of a process or product by which it can be evaluate Standardization is the development and adoption of standards. When they are formulated, standards are not usually the product of a single person, but represent the thoughts and ideas of a group, leavened with the knowledge and information which are currently available. Standards which do not meet certain basic requirements become a hindrance rather than an aid to progress. Standards must not only be correct, accurate, and precise in requiring no more and no less than what is needed for satisfactory results, but they must also be workable in the sense that their usefulness is not nullified by external conditions. Standards should also be acceptable to the people who use them. If they are not acceptable, they cannot be considered to be satisfactory, although they may possess all the other essential characteristics.

22. According to the above paragraph, a processing standard that requires the use of materials that cannot be procured is MOST likely to be   22.___

    A. incomplete   B. unworkable
    C. inaccurate   D. unacceptable

23. According to the above paragraph, the construction of standards to which the performance of job duties should conform is MOST often   23.___

    A. the work of the people responsible for seeing that the duties are properly performed
    B. accomplished by the person who is best informed about the functions involved
    C. the responsibility of the people who are to apply them
    D. attributable to the efforts of various informed persons

24. According to the above paragraph, when standards call for finer tolerances than those essential to the conduct of successful production operations, the effect of the standards on the improvement of production operations is   24.___

    A. negative   B. negligible
    C. nullified   D. beneficial

25. The one of the following which is the MOST suitable title for the above paragraph is   25.___

    A. THE EVALUATION OF FORMULATED STANDARDS
    B. THE ATTRIBUTES OF SATISFACTORY STANDARDS
    C. THE ADOPTION OF ACCEPTABLE STANDARDS
    D. THE USE OF PROCESS OR PRODUCT STANDARDS

KEY (CORRECT ANSWERS)

1.	B	11.	D
2.	A	12.	C
3.	E	13.	B
4.	D	14.	A
5.	E	15.	C
6.	C	16.	B
7.	A	17.	C
8.	D	18.	C
9.	A	19.	B
10.	C	20.	A

21. D
22. C
23. D
24. A
25. B

―――――

ANSWER SHEET

TEST NO. _____ PART _____ TITLE OF POSITION _____
(AS GIVEN IN EXAMINATION ANNOUNCEMENT - INCLUDE OPTION, IF ANY)

PLACE OF EXAMINATION _____ DATE _____
(CITY OR TOWN)   (STATE)

RATING

USE THE SPECIAL PENCIL.   MAKE GLOSSY BLACK MARKS.

#	A B C D E	#	A B C D E	#	A B C D E	#	A B C D E	#	A B C D E
1	∷ ∷ ∷ ∷ ∷	26	∷ ∷ ∷ ∷ ∷	51	∷ ∷ ∷ ∷ ∷	76	∷ ∷ ∷ ∷ ∷	101	∷ ∷ ∷ ∷ ∷
2	∷ ∷ ∷ ∷ ∷	27	∷ ∷ ∷ ∷ ∷	52	∷ ∷ ∷ ∷ ∷	77	∷ ∷ ∷ ∷ ∷	102	∷ ∷ ∷ ∷ ∷
3	∷ ∷ ∷ ∷ ∷	28	∷ ∷ ∷ ∷ ∷	53	∷ ∷ ∷ ∷ ∷	78	∷ ∷ ∷ ∷ ∷	103	∷ ∷ ∷ ∷ ∷
4	∷ ∷ ∷ ∷ ∷	29	∷ ∷ ∷ ∷ ∷	54	∷ ∷ ∷ ∷ ∷	79	∷ ∷ ∷ ∷ ∷	104	∷ ∷ ∷ ∷ ∷
5	∷ ∷ ∷ ∷ ∷	30	∷ ∷ ∷ ∷ ∷	55	∷ ∷ ∷ ∷ ∷	80	∷ ∷ ∷ ∷ ∷	105	∷ ∷ ∷ ∷ ∷
6	∷ ∷ ∷ ∷ ∷	31	∷ ∷ ∷ ∷ ∷	56	∷ ∷ ∷ ∷ ∷	81	∷ ∷ ∷ ∷ ∷	106	∷ ∷ ∷ ∷ ∷
7	∷ ∷ ∷ ∷ ∷	32	∷ ∷ ∷ ∷ ∷	57	∷ ∷ ∷ ∷ ∷	82	∷ ∷ ∷ ∷ ∷	107	∷ ∷ ∷ ∷ ∷
8	∷ ∷ ∷ ∷ ∷	33	∷ ∷ ∷ ∷ ∷	58	∷ ∷ ∷ ∷ ∷	83	∷ ∷ ∷ ∷ ∷	108	∷ ∷ ∷ ∷ ∷
9	∷ ∷ ∷ ∷ ∷	34	∷ ∷ ∷ ∷ ∷	59	∷ ∷ ∷ ∷ ∷	84	∷ ∷ ∷ ∷ ∷	109	∷ ∷ ∷ ∷ ∷
10	∷ ∷ ∷ ∷ ∷	35	∷ ∷ ∷ ∷ ∷	60	∷ ∷ ∷ ∷ ∷	85	∷ ∷ ∷ ∷ ∷	110	∷ ∷ ∷ ∷ ∷

Make only ONE mark for each answer.   Additional and stray marks may be counted as mistakes.   In making corrections, erase errors COMPLETELY.

#	A B C D E	#	A B C D E	#	A B C D E	#	A B C D E	#	A B C D E
11	∷ ∷ ∷ ∷ ∷	36	∷ ∷ ∷ ∷ ∷	61	∷ ∷ ∷ ∷ ∷	86	∷ ∷ ∷ ∷ ∷	111	∷ ∷ ∷ ∷ ∷
12	∷ ∷ ∷ ∷ ∷	37	∷ ∷ ∷ ∷ ∷	62	∷ ∷ ∷ ∷ ∷	87	∷ ∷ ∷ ∷ ∷	112	∷ ∷ ∷ ∷ ∷
13	∷ ∷ ∷ ∷ ∷	38	∷ ∷ ∷ ∷ ∷	63	∷ ∷ ∷ ∷ ∷	88	∷ ∷ ∷ ∷ ∷	113	∷ ∷ ∷ ∷ ∷
14	∷ ∷ ∷ ∷ ∷	39	∷ ∷ ∷ ∷ ∷	64	∷ ∷ ∷ ∷ ∷	89	∷ ∷ ∷ ∷ ∷	114	∷ ∷ ∷ ∷ ∷
15	∷ ∷ ∷ ∷ ∷	40	∷ ∷ ∷ ∷ ∷	65	∷ ∷ ∷ ∷ ∷	90	∷ ∷ ∷ ∷ ∷	115	∷ ∷ ∷ ∷ ∷
16	∷ ∷ ∷ ∷ ∷	41	∷ ∷ ∷ ∷ ∷	66	∷ ∷ ∷ ∷ ∷	91	∷ ∷ ∷ ∷ ∷	116	∷ ∷ ∷ ∷ ∷
17	∷ ∷ ∷ ∷ ∷	42	∷ ∷ ∷ ∷ ∷	67	∷ ∷ ∷ ∷ ∷	92	∷ ∷ ∷ ∷ ∷	117	∷ ∷ ∷ ∷ ∷
18	∷ ∷ ∷ ∷ ∷	43	∷ ∷ ∷ ∷ ∷	68	∷ ∷ ∷ ∷ ∷	93	∷ ∷ ∷ ∷ ∷	118	∷ ∷ ∷ ∷ ∷
19	∷ ∷ ∷ ∷ ∷	44	∷ ∷ ∷ ∷ ∷	69	∷ ∷ ∷ ∷ ∷	94	∷ ∷ ∷ ∷ ∷	119	∷ ∷ ∷ ∷ ∷
20	∷ ∷ ∷ ∷ ∷	45	∷ ∷ ∷ ∷ ∷	70	∷ ∷ ∷ ∷ ∷	95	∷ ∷ ∷ ∷ ∷	120	∷ ∷ ∷ ∷ ∷
21	∷ ∷ ∷ ∷ ∷	46	∷ ∷ ∷ ∷ ∷	71	∷ ∷ ∷ ∷ ∷	96	∷ ∷ ∷ ∷ ∷	121	∷ ∷ ∷ ∷ ∷
22	∷ ∷ ∷ ∷ ∷	47	∷ ∷ ∷ ∷ ∷	72	∷ ∷ ∷ ∷ ∷	97	∷ ∷ ∷ ∷ ∷	122	∷ ∷ ∷ ∷ ∷
23	∷ ∷ ∷ ∷ ∷	48	∷ ∷ ∷ ∷ ∷	73	∷ ∷ ∷ ∷ ∷	98	∷ ∷ ∷ ∷ ∷	123	∷ ∷ ∷ ∷ ∷
24	∷ ∷ ∷ ∷ ∷	49	∷ ∷ ∷ ∷ ∷	74	∷ ∷ ∷ ∷ ∷	99	∷ ∷ ∷ ∷ ∷	124	∷ ∷ ∷ ∷ ∷
25	∷ ∷ ∷ ∷ ∷	50	∷ ∷ ∷ ∷ ∷	75	∷ ∷ ∷ ∷ ∷	100	∷ ∷ ∷ ∷ ∷	125	∷ ∷ ∷ ∷ ∷

ANSWER SHEET

AUG - - 2015

TEST NO. _____ PART _____ TITLE OF POSITION _____
(AS GIVEN IN EXAMINATION ANNOUNCEMENT - INCLUDE OPTION, IF ANY)

PLACE OF EXAMINATION _____ DATE _____
(CITY OR TOWN) (STATE)

RATING

USE THE SPECIAL PENCIL. MAKE GLOSSY BLACK MARKS.

Make only ONE mark for each answer. Additional and stray marks may be counted as mistakes. In making corrections, erase errors COMPLETELY.